COMING HOME

TO THE FATHER WHO LOVES YOU

ROBERT JEFFRESS

WATERBROOK
PRESS

5.46
5/22/07

ED CHRISTNER

COMING HOME
PUBLISHED BY WATERBROOK PRESS
12265 Oracle Boulevard, Suite 200
Colorado Springs, Colorado 80921
A division of Random House, Inc.

Italics in Scripture quotations reflect the author's added emphasis.

Details in some anecdotes and stories have been changed to protect the identities of the persons involved.

ISBN 1-57856-857-9

Published in association with Yates and Yates, LLP, Literary Agent, Orange, California.

Coming Home was originally published by Multnomah Publishers, Inc., in 1997.

Library of Congress Cataloging-in-Publication Data

Jeffress, Robert, 1955–
   Coming home : to the Father who loves you / Robert Jeffress.—2nd ed.
      p. cm.
   Includes bibliographical references.
   ISBN 1-57856-857-9
   1. Spiritual life—Christianity. 2. Prodigal son (Parable) I. Title.
   BV4501.3.J44 2005
   248.8'4—dc22

                              2005019064

Printed in the United States of America
2005—First WaterBrook Press Edition

10 9 8 7 6 5 4 3 2 1

To my daughter, Julia Sue Jeffress,
who makes coming home the highlight of my day

Contents

Acknowledgments

Any successful book is a collaborative effort. I want to express my deepest appreciation to the following people for their help with *Coming Home*.

To Dan Benson, Lisa Lauffer, and Nancy Norris for your keen insights and helpful suggestions that resulted in a better book.

To Mary Ann Tittsworth for her help in proofreading the manuscript.

To my administrative assistant, Carrilyn Baker, for helping me find the time to complete this project.

To my agent, Sealy Yates, for your unfailing friendship and commitment to my ministry.

And finally, to the members of First Baptist Church, Wichita Falls, Texas, for your enthusiastic response to this series and for allowing me the privilege of serving as your pastor.

PART ONE

The Departure

....

CHAPTER 1

A Familiar Story

Why this book is worth your time and money

I don't know you...but then again, I might know you better than you think. If you were motivated enough to purchase this book and then actually open it, I imagine some of the following statements are true about you:

- You can point to a time in your life when you were closer to God than you are now.
- You know you should study your Bible and pray more, but you just don't have the desire.
- You feel overwhelmed by the demands of work and family.
- You feel guilty for thinking about money so much and God so little.
- You find yourself repeating the same mistakes.
- You wonder if your present problems are God's way of getting even with you.
- You're filled with guilt over a past mistake and question whether God can ever forgive you.
- You want to return to the kind of relationship with God you once enjoyed.

Most of us can remember a time when we had a more satisfying relationship with God than we now enjoy. Maybe you can identify with one of the characters in the following story.

DRIFTING

The thought of one more early morning Bible study nauseated Tom Blaylock. He reached to silence the alarm clock so Janet could continue sleeping, and his mind quickly raced over a dozen excuses he could offer for missing the weekly men's gathering: "I overslept," "I had an early morning meeting," "I wasn't feeling well." However, Tom realized that guilt would rob him of the extra hour's sleep, and anyway, he'd face the same battle again next week. As the chairman of the elders in his church, Tom knew he had a responsibility to attend the Bible study each week, but he just didn't want to go. He worried about this, not just because he lacked interest in the men's Bible study, but because he lacked interest in *anything* spiritual.

Tom found it easy to go weeks, or even months, without reading his Bible or spending any significant time in prayer. Every six months a sermon or a barely averted crisis would remind him he needed to make his relationship with God a priority. So he'd resolve to spend thirty minutes each morning in prayer and Bible study. However, the early morning rush around his house or breakfast meetings with his partners at work made that commitment impossible to keep. So Tom decided to have his quiet time at night before he went to bed. Unfortunately, his desire to read the Bible couldn't compete with the sports wrap-up on CNN each evening. By the time the program ended, Tom was too tired to keep his eyes open for three chapters in Obadiah or whatever passage he had on the schedule for that evening.

As Tom struggled to get "blanket victory" that morning, he thought about how different his spiritual life had been twenty years earlier. While in college, he led a campus Bible study every Wednesday at 5:30 A.M., in addition to discipling two other students. During his college years he read through the Bible a half-dozen times and memorized large sections, even entire chapters, of God's Word. He faithfully kept a prayer journal, recording dozens of miraculous answers to his requests. What had happened to him?

He knew the answer, at least part of it. As soon as Tom graduated from college, he and Janet married, and Tom began working as a broker for a regional stock firm. The pressure of a new career took its toll on Tom's spiritual life. In the early years, Tom blamed his seventy- and eighty-hour work-weeks on his God-given responsibility to provide for his family. "Once I become a partner in the firm, I'll never have to worry about money again, and I can start giving renewed attention to my relationship with God."

But now that Tom *had* attained partner status, he recognized the truth: He had become obsessed with work, money, and pleasure. His job as a broker had by necessity focused his attention on money. Spending ten hours a day talking with clients about their 401(k) plans, their estates, and their bulging portfolios naturally caused Tom to think about his own finances. How would he pay for his three children's college educations? Would he have enough money to retire at sixty-five? Should he try to save more aggressively? Tom now devoted every Saturday morning to refiguring the values of his stocks and bonds. If they went up, he felt euphoric. If they declined, he fell into a deep depression. Tom knew that as a Christian he shouldn't focus so much on money, but he couldn't help it. And he blamed his job for his obsession.

Tom's job sabotaged his spiritual life in another way. His long hours allowed him to rationalize his almost insatiable desire for pleasure. When he wasn't daydreaming about his portfolio, he spent his free time plotting his next vacation, golf outing, hunting trip, or out-of-town ball game. "Working as hard as I do, I deserve a break; otherwise, I'll burn out" he reasoned. He even recently read a Christian book that talked about the importance of avoiding workaholism and balancing one's life with relaxation. But deep down Tom knew he had gone overboard and had no idea what to do about it.

Tom's disinterest in his relationship with God hadn't bothered him most of the time, but lately he had been waking up in the middle of the night, thinking about his own mortality. Now in his midforties, Tom realized that he probably had more years behind him than in front of him. Last year's sudden death of a close friend was a frightening reminder that life is fleeting. The fear of dropping dead from a sudden heart attack plagued his thoughts. He didn't fear the *process* of dying, but he was terrified by the *prospect* of facing a God less than pleased with the attention Tom had shown Him these last twenty years.

Janet didn't think much about death and eternity. She had no doubt that she was a Christian and that she would go to heaven when she died. But that seemed a long way off. For now she just wanted to make it through another day without collapsing from exhaustion. Soccer games, tennis practices, church meetings, and school activities coupled with the everyday responsibilities of running a household consumed any extra energy that Janet might have devoted to contemplating life's weightier issues. At least that was how Janet excused the atrophy of her spiritual life.

But, unlike her husband, Janet could point to a specific event on a specific night that turned off the spiritual pilot light in her life. One afternoon as she prepared to take Tom's suits to the cleaners, she discovered a love note from one of Tom's female coworkers. When Tom got home that evening, she confronted him with the note, and he confessed to a short-term affair. She decided to forgive Tom as much for her own benefit and the well-being of her infant son as for her husband's sake.

After several rocky years, everything seemed back on track in their relationship, at least to Tom. But from the time of that discovery fifteen years ago until now, Janet has known that she could never fully trust her husband again. What would prevent him from walking into the bedroom one evening and announcing he was leaving her for another woman?

Even more devastating, Janet has believed that she could never again trust God. If God's plan for her included such heartache and humiliation, what else might His will entail? Her lack of trust in her husband and in God caused her to maintain her emotional distance from both. Although she had never planned to leave Tom or forsake God, the only way Janet has felt she could retain her dignity and maintain her purpose in life was by pouring her life into her children. Although she frequently lamented to friends about her hyperkinetic schedule, Janet had felt grateful that her busyness provided a sense of purpose and an excuse for avoiding a God who disappointed her.

THE GENTLE SLOPE

Some of us, like Janet, can identify a specific incident that drew us away from God: a broken relationship, a lost job, a prolonged illness, an illicit affair, or a bitter disappointment. The majority of us, however, are like Tom, allowing our relationship with God to gradually erode over a long period of time. To paraphrase the words of C. S. Lewis, the road that most often leads a believer away from God is the gradual one—the gentle slope, the soft underfoot, without sudden turnings, without milestones, without signposts. Like Tom, we move away from our Heavenly Father step by step, choice by choice, until one day we awaken in a distant country, far removed from the God we once knew. Why is that?

A. W. Tozer once wrote,

Every farmer knows the hunger of the wilderness. That hunger which no modern farm machinery, no improved agricultural methods can quite destroy. No matter how well-prepared the soil, how well-kept the fences, how carefully painted the buildings, let the owner neglect for awhile his prized and valued acres and they will revert again to the wilds and be swallowed by the jungle or the wasteland. The bias of nature is toward the wilderness never toward the fruitful field.[1]

The same truth applies to our relationship with God. No matter how dramatic our conversion, no matter how sincere our intentions, no matter how saturated we are with doctrine, the bias of life pulls us away from God.

Many years ago, Jesus told a story about a son who allowed his desire for material goods, his thirst for pleasure, and his drive for significance to pull him away from his father. In a moment of temporary insanity, the son demanded his inheritance, departed from his father's home, and dissipated his wealth on wine and women. Only after experiencing a severe crisis did the son come to his senses and long to return to the security of his father's home. How would the father respond to his son's request for forgiveness? Could their relationship ever be the same again? Would the son suffer lasting conse-quences for his rebellion? And what would keep the son from making the same mistake when he again grew tired of his father?

Although some use the prodigal son story to illustrate God's attitude toward non-Christians, I believe that the tale best illustrates God's attitude toward those of us who have allowed our desire for money, pleasure, and ambition to slowly lure us away from our Father. Using the prodigal son story as a backdrop, it is vitally important that we explore together…

- How and why we move away from God and enter the "far country" (it's easier than you think);
- What life is *really* like in the "far country" (it's different than you've been led to believe); and
- How we can return to a vibrant relationship with our Heavenly Father (it's simpler than you imagine).

While we may or may not have fallen into open rebellion against God, many of us have nevertheless grown cold in our faith. God has become a distant deity, a compilation of abstract theological dogma. Although we realize our spiritual condition is not ideal, we wonder, like Tom, if we can ever reclaim the spiritual vitality we once possessed. If you're struggling in these ways, read on and…

- Discover the four reasons we're prone to wander from God;
- Learn the three strategies Satan uses to destroy your spiritual life;
- Apply four principles that will keep you from obsessing about money;
- Find the balance between discipline and recreation;
- Determine when goal setting is right and when it's wrong;
- Understand how God uses crises to get your attention;
- Distinguish between real and false repentance;
- Appreciate the extent of God's forgiveness; and
- Uncover four secrets to maintain consistency in your relationship with God.

At the end of the book, I've included a study guide with questions for each chapter. I encourage you to go through these questions by yourself or with a group to gain the most benefit from the information I've shared.

Above all, like the story of the prodigal son, I want to offer you hope, not condemnation. No matter how far you may have drifted from God, He still loves you and longs for your return.

In his book *Meeting God at a Dead End,* Ron Mehl tells the story of Bob, a connoisseur of garage sales, who resides in Downey, California. One Saturday morning, Bob was at his last stop on his weekly tour of backyard boutiques when he noticed an old motorcycle in the owner's garage. Bob asked the owner how much he would sell the bike for, but the owner tried to dissuade Bob from the purchase, explaining that the motor was frozen and that restoring it would cost as much as a brand-new motorcycle. But Bob persisted, and the owner unloaded it for thirty-five dollars.

A few days passed, and Bob finally found time to call the Harley Davidson Company to research the prices for new parts. Bob gave the salesperson the bike's registration number and, after what seemed an interminable wait, the clerk returned to the phone.

"Uh, sir…I'm going to have to call you back, okay? Could I get your full name, address, and phone number, please?"

Bob gave the clerk the information but was concerned. Had his newfound treasure been involved in an accident, or worse, a crime?

After a few days, Bob received a phone call from a man who introduced himself as an executive with Harley Davidson. The executive said, "Bob, I want you to do something for me. Take the seat off your bike and see if anything is written underneath. Would you do that for me, Bob?"

Bob dutifully laid down the receiver, removed the seat from the bike, then returned to the phone as instructed.

"Yes," Bob replied, "it does have something written there. It's engraved, and it says 'THE KING.'"

After a moment of silence, the executive said, "Bob, my boss has authorized me to offer you $300,000 for that motorcycle. How about it?"

Bob was so startled he couldn't speak. "I'll have to think about it," he replied, and he hung up.

The next day Bob received another phone call. Famed talk-show host and motorcycle enthusiast Jay Leno was on the other end of the line. "Bob," Jay said, "I've heard about your motorcycle and want to offer you $500,000 for it."

You've probably guessed by now why everyone wanted that broken down bucket of rust. The words "THE KING" referred to the King of Rock and Roll himself, Elvis Presley. This motorcycle was worth an unbelievable amount of money, not because of its present condition, but because of the person who had once owned it.[2]

Regardless of your present spiritual condition, the story of the prodigal son can remind you of your incredible value to God because you belong to Him. No matter how far you've strayed, you have a loving Father who watches, waits, and works for your return.

But first, a question: If God values us so much, why does He allow us to wander from Him? As we'll see in the next chapter, a number of forces work to lure us from God and lead us into the far country.

....

CHAPTER 2

Prone to Wander

Satan's three-part blueprint for your destruction

et me tell you about a man named Robert Robinson. Born in England during the eighteenth century, Robinson lost his father while just a boy. His mother, recognizing her inability to support her son, sent him to London to learn the barber trade. While there, Robinson became a Christian through George Whitefield's ministry, and he dedicated his life to preaching the gospel.

When he was only twenty-five, a prestigious Baptist church in Cambridge called Robinson to be its pastor. His fame spread rapidly, and his future seemed unlimited. But at the zenith of his ministry, Robinson fell into immorality, and his star faded almost as quickly as it had appeared.

Many years later, Robert Robinson was traveling by stagecoach and found himself seated next to a woman who was intently reading a passage from a book. The woman asked Robinson to read the passage and share his ideas about its meaning. Robinson read the first few lines:

> Come, Thou Fount of every blessing
> Tune my heart to sing Thy grace;
> Streams of mercy, never ceasing,
> Call for songs of loudest praise...

Robinson looked away and quickly changed the subject. The woman, however, refused to let him off the hook and kept pressuring him for a response. Finally, Robinson broke down and replied, "Madam, I am the poor unhappy man who wrote that hymn many years ago, and I would give a thousand worlds if I had them to enjoy the feelings I had then."

In that well-known hymn, Robert Robinson, either consciously or subconsciously, prophesied his own departure from the faith:

> Prone to wander, Lord, I feel it,
> Prone to leave the God I love;
> Here's my heart, O take and seal it;
> Seal it for thy courts above.[1]

Prone to wander…Prone to *leave* the God I *love*. Many of us have sung that song for so long that we're oblivious to its contradiction. Why would we ever desire to *leave* what we *love?* It doesn't make sense.

LEAVING WHAT WE LOVE

I love going to the movies. I could easily spend all day in a multiplex (and have) going from one screen to another. The saddest part of my cinematic experience is seeing "The End" flash on the screen and realizing that I must return to other responsibilities.

I love spending time with my wife and two daughters. I hate leaving them to catch an airplane for some distant city or even just to go to work. I do it, but I don't like it.

Yet, the hymn writer says that we who genuinely love God also have a genuine desire to depart from Him. We're prone to…

- fall into immoral relationships that destroy our families;
- go weeks and months at a time without talking to God;
- worship temporal possessions instead of our eternal Creator;
- become obsessed with our jobs; and
- renounce our entire belief system at the first hint of unjust suffering.

Why is that? The late Christian businesswoman and entrepreneur Mary Crowley used to make headlines every Christmas in our local newspaper by renting a supermarket for an evening and allowing her employees a one-hour shopping spree to cram as much food into their carts as possible. Sometimes the news media would attend to record those frantic moments of shoppers racing up and down the aisles with a singular purpose.

Imagine someone gave you an empty cart and let you loose for an hour in your favorite department, clothing, or sporting-goods store. After five minutes, your cellular phone rings and your best friend invites you out for pizza. Would you park your basket and leave?

Or imagine that someone announces over the store's public-address system that the president of the United States is at the front of the store and will sign autographs for five minutes. Would you sacrifice those precious minutes of shopping to meet him? I doubt it. Probably very few things could deter you from your primary objective: filling that cart with treasures.

In the same way, God has promised us limitless wealth that will benefit us throughout eternity if we will obey him during the few years He has given us on this planet. "If we endure, we shall also reign with Him" (2 Timothy 2:12). If this is true, why do we allow mundane attractions to so easily distract us from our pursuit of God and His Kingdom? Why, like the prodigal son, would we exchange our place of privilege in our Father's house for pig slop?

Our inclination to wander away from God may be a revolutionary thought for you. Some may dismiss it as rationalization and/or justification for a rebellious attitude toward God. But the spirit of the prodigal can, to some degree, be found in all of us. Let me more fully explain why the human heart is prone to wander.

An Invisible Father

When I was five years old, my father took me to the great State Fair of Texas, a fair with a midway so extraordinary that it was immortalized in the play and movie *State Fair*. As we were about to enter the midway, my dad left for the rest room, instructing me not to move. I stood there and waited for what seemed an eternity. But the appeal of the midway was too strong. The carnival music, the flashing lights, the screams of passengers on the roller coaster lured me from my place of safety. Soon I was caught up in the crowd, far removed from my father. I'll never forget the terror of being surrounded by strangers and not knowing how to return to my dad.

Fortunately, a policeman found me and put me on the back of his three-wheel motorcycle to transport me to the Lost and Found area of the fair. We weaved through the midway crowd as I sat with my back against the officer, my feet dangling over the edge and my tears streaming down my face into the ice cream cone I was licking for comfort. As long as I live I will never forget how I felt when I spotted my dad frantically looking for me in the crowd. When his eyes connected with mine, he galloped toward the racing motorcycle. The policeman, oblivious to what was happening, didn't even notice when my dad reached out and grabbed me from the back of the motorcycle.

Looking back on this frightening experience, my father recognized that he should never have left a five-year-old alone, even for a few moments. But who was responsible for my departure from my father? Certainly, I held the blame for disobeying my father's instructions and wandering away. Had a stranger kidnapped me, I would have suffered the consequences of my disobedience. But without the visible presence of my father to hold me in check, I couldn't resist the midway's attractions. Only the rare five-year-old could have resisted.

Let me be quick to say that our Heavenly Father hasn't abandoned His children. In fact, as Jesus prepared to leave His disciples, He promised to send the Holy Spirit in His absence. "And I will ask the Father, and He will give you another Helper, that He may be with you forever. I will not leave you as orphans; I will come to you" (John 14:16, 18).

Nevertheless, the apostles enjoyed a spiritual advantage that we do not have: They saw, heard, and touched Jesus Christ, the physical manifestation of God. Don't you think that if you had heard Christ's teachings, seen His miracles such as the feeding of the five thousand or His turning water to wine, and witnessed His resurrection and ascension into heaven, you'd be more inclined toward obedience?

I have heard (and taught) that such visible signs do not produce faith. "Just look at the thousands who *didn't* believe," I'd argue. Yet, deep down, I remain unconvinced. It was one thing for the disciples to believe the words of a visible Christ about an invisible world; it is quite a different matter for us two thousand years later to believe the words of an invisible Christ about an invisible world to come. Two thousand years ago, people debated the merit of Christ's teachings; today, people debate whether He said those words or, for that matter, whether He even existed. Perhaps that's why Jesus specifically prayed for those of us who'd be far removed from the events of the first century. "I do not ask in behalf of these alone, but for those also who believe in Me through their word" (John 17:20).

God hasn't shortchanged us in any way; He has given us His Holy Spirit to enlighten us, encourage us, and empower us to live obediently. Nevertheless, we find it easier to be lured away by the bells and whistles of the "midway" than to follow the quiet promptings of the invisible Spirit.

An Active Opponent

My friend and mentor Dr. Howard Hendricks tells of reading an article by General Douglas B. MacArthur, entitled "Requisites for Military Success." The great military leader said that there were four ingredients necessary to win any battle: morale, strength, supply, and knowledge of the enemy. Of the last ingredient, MacArthur said, "The greater the knowledge of the enemy, the greater the potential of victory."[2]

The apostle Paul also expounded on the importance of understanding our enemy. In Ephesians 6:12 he writes, "For our struggle is not against flesh and blood, but against the rulers, against the powers, against the world-forces of this darkness, against the spiritual forces of wickedness in the heavenly places."

Let me point out two obvious, but important, truths in this passage.

1. Living a God-honoring life is difficult. Paul refers to the spiritual life as a "struggle." The word translated "struggle" refers to a wrestling match. When we think about wrestling, we think about those silly farces on television matching "Gorgeous George" against "Python Pete." For all the romping and stomping that goes on in those matches, no one ever seems to get seriously hurt.

But in Paul's day, wrestling was serious business. The "struggle" Paul refers to here was a wrestling match in which the loser had his eyes gouged out and then was killed. It was a life-or-death battle. The apostle uses that imagery to describe the opposition we face in the Christian life. No wonder the Christian landscape is littered with the bodies of believers who have fallen into immorality, materialism, and unbelief. This is no game for sissies.

2. Our greatest obstacle in the Christian life is not another person, but a spiritual power. Paul realized that we all tend to play the blame game. We want to lay our spiritual failures at someone else's feet:

- The mate who doesn't appreciate us;
- The parent who has abused us;
- The employer who underpays us;
- The friend who betrays us; or
- The church member who ignores us.

But Paul says that our real battle in life is against the unseen forces of Satan himself. For this reason, Paul encourages us to "Put on the full armor of God, that you may be able to stand firm against the schemes of the devil" (Ephesians 6:11). Spiritual warfare demands that we use spiritual weapons, and Paul spends the rest of Ephesians 6 describing the spiritual armor available to every Christian.

But the word in Ephesians 6:11 that's relevant to our discussion is "schemes." The Greek word we translate as schemes means methods. Satan has a scheme, a plan, a blueprint for destroying your life. I believe that His detailed blueprint includes:

- the breakup of your marriage;
- the rebellion of your children against God;

- your gradual departure from God; and
- your premature death.

The Bible says that we shouldn't be ignorant of Satan's schemes. How can we discover Satan's strategy for destroying our families, our peace of mind, and our relationships with God? First, we need to study Scripture. As we read the Bible we'll discover that through the ages Satan has used money, pleasure, and ambition to lure believers from God:

- For Judas, it was money—"Those thirty pieces of silver, invested properly, could take care of you in retirement."
- For David, it was pleasure—"You need someone who will meet your needs."
- For Adam and Eve, it was ambition—"You can be like God."
- For Moses, it was also ambition—"You're forty and you've accomplished nothing, so you had better get this exodus rolling."
- For Solomon, it was all three—"You can have it all!"

Lest you think it too simplistic to categorize all of Satan's schemes under just three headings, look at this warning from the apostle John. "Do not love the world, nor the things in the world. If anyone loves the world, the love of the Father is not in him. For all that is in the world, the lust of the flesh [pleasure] and the lust of the eyes [money] and the boastful pride of life [ambition], is not from the Father, but is from the world" (1 John 2:15–16).

In the New Testament, the word translated "world" can mean "that organized system headed by Satan which leaves God out and is a rival to him."[3] John says that since Satan has temporary control over the world system—including Wall Street, Hollywood, and Washington, D.C.—he can effectively employ that system to lure Christians away from God. Specifically, Satan uses money (the lust of the eyes), pleasure (the lust of the flesh), and ambition (the boastful pride of life) to lead believers from their Heavenly Father.

Satan used all three of these tools when he tempted Jesus in the wilderness. For example, Satan appealed to the human materialistic bent by offering Jesus the kingdoms of the world (money). When Jesus was hungry, Satan encouraged him to break his fast and turn the stones into bread (pleasure). When that failed, Satan encouraged Jesus to bypass His Father's plan and reveal Himself as the Messiah (ambition).

When we look at the story of the prodigal son in Luke 15, we find the same three temptations enticing the younger son to leave his father. First, he desired material goods: "Father, give me the share of the estate that falls to me" (v. 12). He had an insatiable desire for pleasure: "He squandered his estate with loose living" (v. 13). And he had the ambition to make a name for himself apart from his father: "And [he] went on a journey into a distant country" (v. 13).

We need to remember that we have an active opponent plotting our destruction. I once heard about a hunter who spent hours tracking a lion on a big-game expedition in Africa. When he finally had his prey cornered and was prepared to pull the trigger, something told him to turn around. To his horror he saw another lion about to pounce on him. The irony is obvious. The hunter had spent hours hunting his prey not realizing that he, too, was being hunted.

We're all hunting something. Some hunt wealth, others hunt indulgence, still others hunt significance. But as we hunt these things, someone hunts us. We have an adversary who is stalking us and will not rest until he completely destroys us. The apostle Peter wrote that our opponent the devil "prowls about like a roaring lion seeking someone to devour" (1 Peter 5:8).

But Satan's ability to spiritually derail us would be severely limited if not for a third factor that makes us prone to wander.

A Fallen Nature

Alypius, the friend and student of Augustine, suffered from a powerful addiction: He was habitually drawn to Rome's bloody gladiator games. This believer knew these games had no place in a Christian's life, so one day he vowed to never attend another game. Weeks went by, and he successfully occupied himself with other activities. But one day Alypius met several friends who, knowing of his weakness for the games, dragged him to the Coliseum. Alypius remained resolute in his vow to not watch the games. He closed his eyes and placed his hands over his ears to block out the frenzied screams of the crowd. But suddenly, the crowd erupted with one piercing scream that penetrated Alypius' covered ears. Unable to overcome his curiosity, he opened his eyes to see a blood-soaked gladiator fall to the ground. To his own horror, Alypius not only watched the scene, he delighted in it. He later confessed to his friend Augustine, "I fell more miserably than that gladiator."[4]

All of us can identify and sympathize with Alypius. How many times have we resolved, "God, I will *never* do this again," only to find ourselves not only repeating the forbidden action but *loving* it? The apostle Paul vividly described the internal battle we all face:

> No matter which way I turn I can't make myself do right. I want to but I can't. When I want to do good, I don't; and when I try not to do wrong, I do it anyway. Now if I am doing what I don't want to, it is plain where the trouble is: sin still has me in its evil grasp.
>
> It seems to be a fact of life that when I want to do what is right, I inevitably do what is wrong. I love to do God's will so far as my new nature is concerned; but there is something else deep within me, in my lower nature, that is at war with my mind and wins the fight and makes me a slave to the sin that is still within me. (Romans 7:18–23, TLB)

Now for just a few pages we are going to talk theology. Before your eyes glaze over, or before you put down this book and turn on *Wheel of Fortune*, let me assure you that this theology relates directly to your life.

In the above passage, Paul claims that the key to understanding your inclination toward evil is understanding a potent inner power called your sin nature. That sin nature acts like a magnet pulling you away from God. James, the half-brother of Jesus, gives us further insight into how our sin nature works. "Let no one say when he is tempted, 'I am being tempted by God;' for God cannot be tempted by evil, and He Himself does not tempt anyone. But each one is tempted when he is carried away and enticed by his own lust" (James 1:13–14).

James has in mind a Christian on the brink of falling into sin who, before taking the final plunge, offers this excuse: "Since we serve a sovereign God, He must be responsible for this temptation. Who am I to resist His power?" James says that is a lame rationalization. God doesn't tempt us.

Interestingly, James doesn't even use the old Flip Wilson argument: "The devil made me do it." Yes, Satan actively seeks our destruction, but he wouldn't have much power over us if we didn't have cravings for sin—lusts. James says that we are carried away and enticed by these inward cravings. The word we translate as "carried away" means "to be drawn by an inward power."

As I write these words, it's almost noon, and I have a strong inward desire drawing me away from this computer and toward a barbecue joint down the street. And I confess, I am about to succumb to that strong inward power! But the kind of craving James describes isn't a harmless desire for food but a strong inward pull toward things outside of God's will for our lives. Our sin nature pulls us toward those things and entices us. Enticed is a fishing term that means "hooked." James employs a word picture of a fish so blinded by its desire for food that it snaps at the bait, not realizing that the bait contains a hook that will destroy it.

Any good fisherman knows that you use different bait for different types of fish. In the same way, every Christian is enticed by different "bait," and Satan is a master fisherman who knows which bait will hook us. For example, a Christian who finds sexual and emotional satisfaction in his or her marriage probably won't be easily tempted by an illicit relationship. However, an illegal business deal that promises to satisfy a craving for money might hook this person. We need to study ourselves so that we can identify those areas that make us vulnerable to temptation.

In a church I used to pastor, a certain businessman loved to debate theology with me. He was particularly hung up on the issue of a Christian's sin nature. "I don't believe a Christian has a sin nature," he'd say. "Romans 6 clearly teaches that our sin nature was destroyed when we became Christians. Your kind of teaching leads to a defeated Christian life and gives believers a great excuse to sin." I remember sitting for hours arguing this subject without ever convincing my friend that he possessed a powerful sin nature that he would always have to battle.

In fairness to my friend and others who may wonder about this issue, let's determine what Romans 6 says about sin's power over a Christian's life. "Knowing this, that our old self was crucified with Him, that our body of sin might be done away with, that we should no longer be slaves to sin; for he who has died is freed from sin" (Romans 6:6–7).

My friend argued that a Christian has only one set of desires, not two. When we become Christians our sin natures, inherited from Adam, are destroyed or crucified. If our sin natures continue to flourish, then what did Christ's death accomplish for us? And how do we understand Paul's words in Romans 6?

Good questions, to be sure. But the Bible provides good answers to those questions. Let's look at other passages of Scripture to help us interpret these verses. As we examine Paul's writings, we'll find that he consistently teaches that Christians struggle with their sin natures. For example, consider these passages:

> But I say, walk by the Spirit, and you will not carry out the desire of the flesh. For the flesh sets its desire against the Spirit, and the Spirit against the flesh; for these are in opposition to one another, so that you may not do the things that you please. (Galatians 5:16–17)

> That, in reference to your former manner of life, you lay aside the old self, which is being corrupted in accordance with the lusts of deceit. And put on the new self which in the likeness of God has

been created in righteousness and holiness of the truth. (Ephesians 4:22, 24)

But now you also, put them all aside: anger, wrath, malice, slander, and abusive speech from your mouth. Do not lie to one another, since you laid aside the old self with its evil practices, and have put on the new self who is being renewed to a true knowledge according to the image of the One who created Him. (Colossians 3:8–10)

Whether you want to label them *flesh* and *spirit* or the *old self* and the *new self,* the forces of good and evil wage a civil war in your heart. Christ's death on the cross did not eliminate sin's *influence* in your life, but it did destroy sin's *absolute power* over your life. If that sounds like a bunch of theological mumbo jumbo, consider this story that my friend Bobb Biehl tells about a day he spent working in the circus:

When we got there, it was a hot, dusty, windy day at the fairgrounds where the circus was playing. We moved props from one of the three rings to the next, helped in any way we could, and generally got dusty, dirty, tired, and hungry.

During one of the breaks, I started chatting with the man who trains the animals for Hollywood movies. "How is it that you can stake down a ten-ton elephant with the same size stake that you use for this little fellow?" I asked. The "little fellow" weighed about three hundred pounds.

"It's easy when you know two things: Elephants really do have great memories, but they really aren't very smart. When they are babies, we stake them down. They try to tug away from the stake maybe ten thousand times before they realize that they can't possibly get away. At that point their 'elephant memory' takes over and they remember for the rest of their lives that they can't get away from the stake."[5]

I believe that Paul's words in Romans 6 mean that Christ has freed us from sin's power in our lives. Sin has no more control over a Christian than a small stake has over a ten-ton elephant. Once we become Christians, we have an incredible power to say no to sin—but we must act in a way consistent with that power. For this reason, Paul writes: "Even so consider yourselves to be dead to sin, but alive to God in Christ Jesus. Therefore do not let sin reign in your mortal body that you should obey its lusts" (Romans 6:11–12). Although we're no longer slaves to our sin nature, we should never forget its presence within us.

I remember hearing my former pastor Dr. W. A. Criswell tell the story about a hunter in India trapped in a torrential downpour. The great river near his hunting ground overflowed, and he escaped to a little island of high ground. While he temporarily lodged there, a tiger swam through the swift current and landed on the little island. The tiger looked wet, afraid, and cowed like a domestic cat. The hunter's first instinct was to care for the frightened tiger and feed it. But the hunter eventually came to his senses and shot the tiger.

Many people would label the hunter's action as cruel, but the hunter was wiser than his critics. He had sense enough to know that after a while, when the tiger grew hungry, the hunter would be the catch of the day. Even if the tiger behaved for a while, his carnivorous nature would take over, and he'd eventually eat the man. It was the nature of the beast.

Dr. Criswell then makes this application: We all have within us a latent ability to commit any sin. Most murders aren't premeditated but happen in anger and fury. Why? Because we're born with a sin nature. Unfortunately, unlike the hunter, we can't once and for all rid ourselves of the beast within. As long as we live, we'll battle against an active opponent who will use man's fallen nature and its desires to lure us from our Heavenly Father.

If all of this discussion about whether or not a Christian has a sin nature seems academic rather than practical, let me share with you how my theological debate with my former church member resolved itself. My friend, who refused to believe that a Christian still possesses a sin nature, decided one day that he was tired of being married. He believed that his family responsibilities hindered his ability to reach his full potential at work. The morning that his wife delivered their fifth child, he announced that he was leaving. From all reports, he has renounced everything he once believed.

Understanding the reality of our sin nature and the resolve of our spiritual enemy is the first line of defense against our defection from the faith.

Now that we've completed our brief theology lesson, we need to get extremely practical. Exactly how does the Enemy use money, pleasure, and ambition to slowly lead us from our Father and into the far country?

....

CHAPTER 3

Money Mania

Why it is so easy to worship money

Howard Dayton tells the story of a young man named Roger Morgan who emerged from the Appalachian Mountains with one resolve in his heart: to make a fortune. Money soon became his all-consuming passion in life, and over a period of years he accumulated several million dollars. However, the Great Depression wiped out his portfolio and reduced him to a life of poverty.

Without a dime to his name, Roger Morgan wandered through the country trying to eke out a living any way he could. One day a fellow hobo found Morgan standing on the Golden Gate Bridge staring into the icy water below. The hobo suggested that Morgan step from the dangerous precipice so they could talk. "Leave me alone," Morgan insisted. "I'm trying to think. There is something more important in life than money...but I've forgotten what it is."[1]

That is the danger of money. Whether you have a lot or a little, money has a way of consuming all your attention and affection. Most of us know people whose desire for money and material goods has caused them to neglect their family responsibilities, engage in illegal and unethical conduct, or plunge into ill-advised investment schemes. Perhaps you've even fallen into one of these traps yourself. The insatiable desire for money has destroyed friendships, marriages, and even churches.

But I believe that the most dangerous attribute of the love of money is its ability to lead us away from our Heavenly Father. In his book *I Talk Back to the Devil,* C. S. Lewis writes, "Money often comes between men and God. Someone has said that you can take two small ten-cent pieces, just two dimes, and shut out the view of a panoramic landscape. Go to the mountains and just hold two coins closely in front of your eyes—the mountains are still there, but you cannot see them at all because there is a dime shutting off the vision in each eye."

I believe that is why Jesus said, "No one can serve two masters. Either he will hate the one and love the other, or he will be devoted to the one and despise the other. You cannot serve God and Money" (Matthew 6:24, NIV).

Think about that statement for a moment. Notice what it *doesn't* say. Jesus did not say, you cannot serve God and…

sex or

sports or

work or

another person.

He *did* say that we can't serve God and money. Why? While we can allow another person, a career, recreational pursuits, or sensual activity to become an idol to us, Jesus understood that money holds a unique power over us. Perhaps when Jesus spoke these words, He had in mind the rich young ruler who would reject Him because of money or His disciple Judas Iscariot who would betray Him for thirty pieces of silver. In both cases these men traded their eternal souls for temporal gain. Money can cause an otherwise rational person to make irrational choices.

This week a large metropolitan newspaper carried the horrific story of a brutal murder that took place in a fashionable suburb. In the middle of the night, an intruder slashed through a screened window and viciously stabbed to death two boys, a five-year-old and a six-year-old. According to the mother's report, the intruder then tried to kill her while her husband and another baby slept upstairs.

However, after weeks of investigation, police charged the mother with committing these two murders. Why? Many believe that the desire for wealth spurred her on. The couple had enjoyed a nice home, expensive clothes, costly hobbies. However, some recent economic downturns had threatened that lifestyle. Some suspect that the mother hoped to collect on an insurance policy taken out on both boys' lives, so she brutally murdered her two sons.

Make no mistake about it, money has the power to motivate rational people to make irrational choices. Just consider the story of the prodigal son. This boy enjoyed the kind of life that most of us can only dream about. He lived in a luxurious home, servants waited on him around the clock, and he enjoyed the assurance that one day he'd inherit a fortune. Yet, he had an unquenchable desire to get his hands on his father's cash:

> A certain man had two sons; and the younger of them said to his father, "Father, give me the share of the estate that falls to me." And he divided his wealth between them. And not many days later, the younger son gathered everything together and went on a journey into a distant country and there he squandered his estate with loose living. (Luke 15:11–13)

What motivated the younger son to leave home? Although a strained relationship with his older brother, his obsession with making his own mark in the world, or the absence of a strong and loving mother could have been factors in his decision to leave home, his primary reason for moving away was money. He knew that his dad had a stockpile of wealth that would one day be his. But he couldn't wait for his father to die. He wanted his money *now*.

Although Jesus doesn't provide us with the details of the father and son's conversation, one can only imagine the range of emotions the father experienced. I imagine that the father initially responded with outrage: "You want me to do *what*? After all that I have done for you, how could you ask such a thing?"

But that outrage eventually turned to deep hurt. When the father realized that his son only wanted the wealth he could provide, he quietly liquidated his assets and divided the estate according to Jewish custom: two-thirds to the older son (who probably refused to take his portion) and one-third to the younger son.

What is it about money that would cause this son to alienate his powerful but loving father and leave the comfort and security of a luxurious home? Come to think of it, why do *any* of us allow money to occupy such a prominent position in our minds and hearts? Let me point out four alluring qualities of money:

Money promises security for the future

Yesterday a friend called to tell me about a mutual acquaintance who just made $25 million on a business deal. After paying some bills and buying a few toys, our friend deposited $15 million in the bank. Can you imagine how secure you'd feel if you had $15 million in the bank? You'd never have to…

- worry what your employer thought of you;
- wonder where your next meal was coming from;
- concern yourself with the high cost of providing a college education for your children; or
- wonder if you'll have to eat oatmeal during your retirement years.

And yet, for all the supposed security that money offers, it still cannot protect us from many adversities. One of the most powerful illustrations of this truth is a story Jesus once told about a man who mistakenly thought that money could protect him from every misfortune in life.

To understand the parable of the rich fool found in Luke 12, we must first understand the historical context. Jesus was on his way to Jerusalem to be crucified. He had just warned his followers about the strong persecution they could expect to endure. But in the crowd was someone who had no regard for God's kingdom. Instead, he had a more pressing concern: getting his share of his father's estate. In fact, he wanted Jesus to settle the dispute with his brother immediately. Jesus replied with words I have often used when church members want me to settle their petty disagreements, such as who should receive a key to the church kitchen: "Man, who appointed Me a judge or arbiter over you?" (Luke 12:14).

But before Jesus turned His back on the young man, He pointed out a root problem He detected in this man's heart: greed. "Beware, and be on your guard against every form of greed; for not even when one has an abundance does his life consist of his possessions" (Luke 12:15).

Sometimes, we read that statement without allowing its meaning to penetrate our hearts. Think about it for a moment. You can't measure your life by your possessions. How contrary that truth is to our thinking today. Recently *Money* magazine carried a feature story entitled "Determining Your Net Worth." The article encouraged readers to calculate their net worth by adding the value of their assets (stocks, bonds, cash, real estate, jewelry, etc.) and subtracting their liabilities (bank loans, credit-card balances, home mortgages, etc.). The resulting number is your net worth. The article then enabled you to compare your net worth with others in your same age and income brackets.

Such an exercise results in mixed emotions. How much you really own may surprise you, especially as you compare yourself to others who have less. You may suddenly feel wealthy enough to splurge on a vacation, clothes, or a new car. On the other hand, you may look at those on the survey who have *more* than you. Suddenly you feel poorer than you did just a moment ago, and you could slide into a deep depression, although nothing has really changed about your financial condition.

But such an accounting fails to take into consideration how easily we can lose our net worth. To illustrate this truth, Jesus told this story: "The land of a certain rich man was very productive. And he began reasoning to himself, saying, 'What shall I do, since I have no place to store my crops?' And he said, 'This is what I will do: I will tear down my barns and build larger ones, and there I will store all my grain and my goods. And I will say to my soul, "Soul, you have many goods laid up for many years to come; take your ease, eat, drink and be merry"'" (Luke 12:16–19).

This guy had a *problem* that the rest of humanity would die for: He had too much! He lay awake at night worrying about what he would do with his abundance. He had a number of choices. He could have called his family together for a service of thanksgiving to God. He could have given some of his money to support God's work or to help those less fortunate than himself. He might have begun to divide his estate among his heirs.

Instead, he chose to worship his money.

To worship money means to ascribe attributes to money that rightfully belong to God alone. In this case, worshiping money meant believing that money provided protection from future problems in life. Therefore, the rich fool began to stockpile his wealth so: (a) He'd never have to depend on anyone else for his future security; and (b) He could quit work and lead a life of luxury. Please note that *neither* of these goals corresponds with God's plan for our lives.

First, God wants us to trust Him, not our money, for the future. King Solomon wrote: "Give me neither poverty nor riches, but give me only my daily bread. Otherwise, I may have too much and disown you and say, 'Who is the LORD?'" (Proverbs 30:8–9, NIV).

Solomon understood from personal experience how a stockpile of money can lead people from God. His insatiable desire for women and wealth caused him to turn from God (1 Kings 11:1–5). God had expressly prohibited the kings of Israel from hoarding large amounts of silver or gold (Deuteronomy 17:17), and David's and Solomon's refusals to obey these commands led to their downfalls.

Second, God never meant for us to quit working and lead lives of luxury as this rich fool desired to do. Spending the last twenty or thirty years of your life with no greater purpose than self-fulfillment is a surefire formula for spiritual disaster. Yes, I realize that the idea of retirement is ingrained in our cultural psyche, but such an idea is unscriptural and can lead us away from God.

Although the rich fool trusted in his wealth to provide a luxurious life and protect him from life's uncertainties, he failed to consider one contingency: his own death. "But God said to him, 'You fool! This very night your soul is required of you; and now who will own what you have prepared?'" (Luke 12:20).

As powerful as money is, it can't protect you from everything. For example, money can't protect you from a stranger who steals your mate's affection and dissipates your wealth. Money can't protect you from a lawsuit that instantly wipes out your nest egg. Money can't protect you from a job loss that depletes your savings. And money can't protect you from a blood clot or a tumor that sends you to your Maker, stripped of all of your possessions.

Let's be honest. Money can protect us from *some* problems in life. Just a few moments ago I opened a letter from one of our low-income members who is suffering tremendous medical problems and doesn't have the money to purchase much-needed medication. Those who can afford insurance or who have a cash reserve don't experience that kind of problem. In fact, we have difficulty understanding the anxiety that this kind of poverty produces. Proverbs 10:15 reminds us that "The rich man's wealth is his fortress; the ruin of the poor is their poverty."

Both the parable of the rich fool and our everyday experiences remind us that money has limited power to protect us. Proverbs 11:4 also reminds us that "Wealth is worthless in the day of wrath" (NIV).

Money relieves stress

Another reason we allow money to capture our affections is its promise to alleviate stress in our lives. My friend who experienced the $25 million windfall had lived for fifteen years with a $10 million debt hanging over his head. Can you imagine the pressure that kind of debt would produce? Many people today live under the pressure of debt. In March of 1997 the American Bankers Association reported that credit-card delinquencies were at an all-time high. According to VeriBanc, the United States had $223 billion in outstanding credit-card debt in 1996, up from $172 billion in 1994. Personal bankruptcies are also at an all-time high. In 1996, new bankruptcy cases surpassed one million for the first time. And recent surveys have shown that most Americans could not survive more than four weeks without a job.

I recently came across a newspaper article that vividly illustrates the financial pressure most people feel. Since their inception in the 1940s, game shows have given contestants hope of winning new cars, glamorous wardrobes, exotic vacations, or piles of cash. Viewers vicariously experience the thrill of receiving mountains of money that can solve their financial woes.

In recent years, a new game show premiered that offers contestants the hope of leaving with...nothing. The show is called *Debt*. Listen to this hilarious description of the show:

> First, there is the central premise of the show, explained in the opening. A woman languishes at a desk covered with bills while a voice booms, "Are you drowning in debt?" Suddenly she is picked up by a giant hand that belongs to [the host]. "Then it's time to play *Debt* [the host] proclaims as he drops the woman in a cloud. "The game show where three debt-laden Americans just like you compete to have us pay off all their bills and go home with nothing."[2]

Today, many Americans feel so stressed by their bills that they embrace a game show that promises them nothing except freedom from crushing debt!

But while an infusion of cash can greatly relieve stress, money can also induce stress. The low-income earner doesn't concern him- or herself with the Dow Jones Industrial Average. The street person doesn't worry whether or not the Federal Reserve Board will raise interest rates. The consumer with a zero net worth doesn't fret that one day somebody might sue him or her, wiping out his or her savings.

King Solomon, the wealthiest man who ever lived, offered this insight about money: "As goods increase, so do those who consume them. And what benefit are they to the owner except to feast his eyes on them? The sleep of a laborer is sweet, whether he eats little or much, but the abundance of a rich man permits him no sleep" (Ecclesiastes 5:11–12, NIV).

Having experienced great wealth, Solomon reminds us that money can sometimes provide more problems than solutions.

Money can fulfill our desires

I have a friend who once encouraged me to make a list of ten things I wanted to do before I died. Take a few moments and do the same thing.

If your list looks anything like mine, you've jotted down some spiritual, vocational, and relational goals, but you've included some pleasure-oriented desires as well. I've listed trips I want to take, clothes I'd like to wear, the kind of home I'd like to live in, and the type of automobile I'd like to drive. Right or wrong, I have these desires.

What is the one thing that stands between me and those desires? Money. If only I had X number of dollars I could...

- build that home;
- drive that car;
- take that trip;
- wear those clothes.

Is it any wonder that we are fascinated with money? Money allows us to fulfill the desires of our short and fleeting lives.

Yet, just as money can help us fulfill legitimate desires, it can also plunge us into harmful pursuits. Paul wrote, "But those who want to get rich fall into temptation and a snare and many foolish and harmful desires which plunge men into ruin and destruction" (1 Timothy 6:9).

Notice the two kinds of desires linked to money.

Foolish Desires: Let's translate *foolish* as frivolous. I think of one man I know who was near bankruptcy. He was so destitute that his family didn't have enough to eat. He prayed that the Lord would answer his pleading for help. The Lord responded to his prayers, and almost overnight made this man a millionaire. How did this man use his money? He bought a lake house, took up golf, built a luxurious home, obtained a membership at the local country club, became an avid hunter, and enrolled his children in every extracurricular activity available.

Over a period of several years, this man and his family have dropped out of church. They are too busy on the weekends to attend. Money has been the passport to a life of frivolous desires.

Harmful desires: Let's be fair to those who own lake houses, play golf, belong to country clubs, hunt, and engage their children in music lessons and sports. You can certainly do all of those things and maintain an intimate relationship with God, carefully balancing leisure with other responsibilities. However, Paul says that money not only tempts us with frivolous desires but with harmful desires. Money can lead us from God by tempting us to participate in activities contrary to His will.

A friend of mine had been married for ten years to an exceptional Christian woman, and they had three small children. While attending an industry convention in another city, my friend met an attractive woman. Although nothing immoral occurred that weekend, when the man returned home, he began calling this woman on the phone. After several months, they decided to rendezvous in a distant city for a weekend affair. Over the following three years, this man spent more than twenty thousand dollars pursuing this woman with flowers, gifts, phone calls, and frequent out-of-town trips. This man's wealth allowed him to fulfill lusts that eventually cost him his family. Money's ability to fulfill our desires is a two-edged sword.

Money can provide us with independence

Imagine the following scenario for a moment. For twenty years you've labored at a job that you mostly enjoy but has also been frustrating. During those years, you have, at times, been so bored that you could barely motivate yourself to crawl out of bed on Monday mornings. Other times your insensitive boss has enraged you. Occasionally the rumor of a company merger has made you fearful of losing your job.

For two decades, you've experienced a love/hate relationship with your job. Then one day (a) your rich Aunt Ethel dies, (b) you win the lottery, or

(c) make up your own fantasy, and you instantly become a millionaire. What would you do about your job? Would you tell your boss what you really think of him and quit immediately? Or would you continue in your job with a renewed zeal knowing that...

- you didn't have to go to work if you didn't want to;
- you could tell your boss to take a flying leap whenever you had the inclination; and
- you never had to worry about the effects of losing your job.

Studies have shown that most of us would choose the second option. Why? For several reasons: the desire to be productive, the identity we derive from our jobs, and the need to interact with other people. Most of us would love the luxury of continuing our work while maintaining our sense of independence.

Yet the independent spirit that wealth engenders isn't always healthy. I know of a pastor who, early in his ministry, went through a very hurtful experience. He and his small family moved to their first church. The membership provided the pastor with a parsonage and a small allowance for refurbishing the parsonage with new carpeting and a new coat of paint. The pastor, fully believing he had the authority to do so, contracted for the work to be done. He didn't understand that the church expected to vote on any and every detail of the refurbishing. When the church members heard that the pastor had the work done without their approval, they dismissed him from his job.

This pastor was so outraged and hurt over the experience that he made this vow to himself: He would remain in the ministry, but he would become so wealthy that he'd never again have to listen to anyone.

Over the years, he built a thriving ministry. Many believed he was the finest Bible teacher they had ever heard. He pastored larger and larger churches and built a large television ministry. But he was obsessed with money. He began every day by reading the stock-market report rather than the Bible. Those who became close to him were astonished at how his conversation rarely involved spiritual concerns and often involved financial matters. His relentless pursuit of money allowed him to amass a small fortune, but it also destroyed his ministry.

Whenever anyone offered any criticism about the church or the pastor personally, he cut that person to shreds with his sharp tongue. He often made decisions about the church independently from his board of elders or congregation. When challenged about those decisions, he sarcastically replied, "You're free to fire me anytime you wish. I don't need your money."

One day, however, the church accepted his challenge. In a called meeting, the congregation dismissed him as pastor. Although my friend will never have to worry about starving to death, his desire for independence has caused him to forfeit his ministry. One of the most potent dangers of money is the freedom it offers, freedom we can use for good or evil.

Now let's review for a moment everything money can provide: security for the future, removal of stress, fulfillment of desires, and independence from drudgery. Is it any surprise that money can so easily consume our thoughts and affections? No relationship, job, sensual experience, or recreational pursuit offers all of the above. Maybe that's why Jesus pointed to money as the number one contender against God for our affections.

Perhaps you've allowed money to lure you from God. As you honestly evaluate your thoughts and affections, you realize you're obsessed with making, spending, or saving the stuff. You recognize that your preoccupation with money has slowly strangled your love for God. You want to change your attitude about money and rekindle your love for God, but you don't know what to do. After all, we still need money to live.

How can a Christian possess money without being possessed by it? We'll focus on that question in the next chapter.

....

Money Sense

How to use money without loving it

S aint Francis of Assisi understood how money can lure a Christian away from God. So he instructed his friars not to touch it. One day, a worshiper left a coin at the base of the sanctuary cross. When one of Francis's friars saw the coin, he picked it up and threw it on the window sill. When Francis discovered that the friar had touched the coin, he strongly rebuked the friar then commanded him to lift the coin from the window sill with his lips, find a pile of donkey dung, and with his lips, drop the coin into the refuse.[1]

After reading the last chapter, you may realize that the love of (or, at least, preoccupation with) money has drawn you away from God. You genuinely desire to shift your affection from the temporal to the eternal, but you don't know how to do it.

How should Christians view money? Must we feel the same disdain for it as Saint Francis, or do we have another alternative? Contrary to popular thinking, the Bible offers a much more enlightened and balanced view than that of Saint Francis. As I search God's Word, I find three important principles about money.

1. We must use money without worshiping it

In talking about the evils of money, someone once pointed out that money caused:

- the rich farmer to deceive himself into thinking all was well;

- the rich young ruler to reject Christ;
- the rich man to neglect Lazarus;
- Judas to betray the Lord Jesus Christ; and
- Ananias and Sapphira to lie to the Holy Spirit.

True. But we should also remember that money:

- built Solomon's temple where people could worship God;
- provided the food for the Last Supper;
- supported Paul's three missionary journeys;
- fed the poor saints in Jerusalem; and
- promoted the spread of the gospel throughout the world.

Unfortunately, we find it difficult to maintain a balanced view of money. We either love it or loathe it. Dallas Willard uses John Wesley as an example of a Christian who hated money because of its corrupting influence. Willard points out that many of Wesley's followers came from a lower socioeconomic background. When they applied Wesley's simple principles about frugality, saving, work, and stewardship, they became prosperous. Their prosperity, in turn, led to selfishness and self-indulgence. Thus, Wesley concluded, "true, scriptural Christianity has a tendency, in the process of time, to undermine and destroy itself."[2] Willard observes, "For all of Wesley's religious genius— and it was great—he could not understand the possibility of a Christian teaching and discipline that would produce people capable of holding possessions and power without being corrupted by them."[3]

Let's give Wesley some credit. The track record for people using wealth without worshiping it isn't great. But it can be done. The apostle Paul held out that possibility when he wrote: "Instruct those who are rich in this present world not to be conceited or to fix their hope on the uncertainty of riches, but on God, who richly supplies us with all things to enjoy" (1 Timothy 6:17).

Yes, Paul conceded, money can lead to pride and idolatry. However, we can't solve the money dilemma by divesting ourselves of all our possessions. Poverty does not produce godliness. The poor can worship money just as easily as the wealthy. Instead, we must shift our affections from money to God. We don't make this decision once and for all; we continually fight this battle. But we *can* win it.

2. We must save money without hoarding it

Solomon wrote that he had witnessed (and maybe even experienced) "riches being hoarded by their owner to his hurt" (Ecclesiastes 5:13). To stockpile cash like the rich fool of Luke 12 is harmful. Nevertheless, the Bible does teach that Christians should regularly save money.

Recently I was interviewed on a radio talk show. A listener posed this question: "When you talk about saving money, aren't you encouraging people to trust their bank accounts instead of God for their future needs?" That is certainly a legitimate concern, but the Bible consistently teaches the importance of saving money.

What are the biblical reasons for saving money?

a. To provide for our future needs—Jack is forty-two years old and earns sixty thousand dollars a year. Although he doesn't spend his money extravagantly, he drives a Jeep Cherokee, lives in a nice home, and enjoys a luxury vacation once a year. His employer provides no retirement benefits, and this distresses Jack. Nevertheless, between his family's needs and his occasional spending splurges (like the new laptop computer he bought last week), Jack finds it difficult to save for the future. Whenever he begins to worry about his retirement years, he comforts himself by remembering God's faithfulness in providing for past needs. That same God will take care of Jack in the future…he hopes.

Yes, God wants to provide for our future needs. But *how* does He do so? God has already revealed His retirement plan in the Bible. He commands us to regularly set aside a portion of our current income to fund future expenditures. Listen to Solomon's words. Even though the old king enjoyed having a good time with his money, he also understood the importance of saving for the future: "Go to the ant, O sluggard. Observe her ways and be wise, which, having no chief, officer or ruler, prepares her food in the summer, and gathers her provision in the harvest. How long will you lie down, O sluggard? When will you arise from your sleep?" (Proverbs 6:6–9).

Even a creature as small as an ant realizes that harvest time doesn't last forever, so he sets aside food for winter. The same principle applies to us. Even if we never lose our jobs, our working days are still numbered. How can we prepare for those times when we have no steady stream of income? God's plan is for us to set aside some of our current income to fund our future needs.

In my book *Guilt-Free Living* I relate the story about the origin of the 401(k) retirement plan. Theodore Benna was a thirty-eight-year-old consultant for an employee-benefits firm in Philadelphia. Yet the fifteen years he had spent on the job left him unfulfilled. Benna was a devout Christian who wanted to use his job to glorify God. He says that through prayer God opened his eyes to a little known provision in the Internal Revenue Code, section 401(k), that would allow employees to defer some of their income and place it into retirement plans. Benna made this discovery more than twenty years ago. Today, millions of workers will enjoy secure retirements because they take advantage of 401(k) plans.[4]

Instead of expecting money to suddenly drop like manna from heaven or hoping for a rich uncle to remember us in his will, we should understand God wants us to save a portion of our income to provide for our future income needs.

Let me give you some practical suggestions here. Find out whether you're eligible to contribute to an Individual Retirement Account (IRA) which is a way to allow your retirement dollars to grow on a tax-deferred basis. If you are eligible, consider opening an IRA, and set up a plan for making regular deposits. If your company offers a 401(k) plan, contribute the maximum amount possible to it. If you're self-employed, have your accountant set up a SEP (Self-Employed Pension) plan. I believe God can use such plans to provide for our needs.

b. To provide for our families' current needs—Paul wrote, "But if anyone does not provide for his own, and especially for those of his household, he has denied the faith, and is worse than an unbeliever" (1 Timothy 5:8).

Many have used that verse as an exhortation for men to find jobs so they can provide for the basic needs of their families. But the context of that verse is taking care of one's parents and grandparents in their old age so that they aren't burdens to others.

Imagine the following situation. You have two kids in college, a mortgage, and car payments, and you suddenly discover that you'll have to assume responsibility for your parents' nursing-home bill. Could you survive financially? If so, for how long?

As life spans increase, many middle-aged couples find themselves in the triple bind of funding their children's education, saving for their own retirement, and caring for aged parents. Few people can fund those costs out of present income alone. That's why saving is imperative.

c. To protect against adversity—It doesn't take a rocket scientist to figure out that we will have future retirement and family needs to fund. We can all see that. But what about the unseen needs that suddenly ambush us?

Jerry had spent all of his working life in the banking industry. Over the course of twenty years, he had risen from the position of teller to that of senior vice president. He and his family enjoyed the benefits of an above-average income. Nevertheless, Jerry had been concerned about his industry's instability. Therefore, in addition to his pension account, Jerry began setting aside additional income in case he was suddenly laid off.

Last year, Jerry was called to the holding company's headquarters and told that his bank was merging with another. As a result, his position was eliminated. His superiors gave him two months' salary as severance pay and a letter of commendation for twenty years of service. That was it! Two months after Jerry's layoff, his teenage son was diagnosed with cancer. His son's only hope of survival was a year of extensive (and expensive) treatment at a cancer hospital in another state.

In spite of these two catastrophic events, Jerry and his family have remained extraordinarily calm. Even though Jerry's search for a new job has been fruitless and his family has incurred mounting medical expenses, they have not panicked. Why? They would quickly acknowledge God's gifts of supernatural peace and provision for their material needs. But had Jerry not wisely set aside a portion of his income during the good times, I doubt that he and his family would have remained so calm this past year. Their savings has been a harbor during the storms of adversity.

We must strike a delicate balance between trusting in savings and trusting in God for our needs. Nevertheless, we should understand that one of the primary methods God uses to provide for our unexpected needs is through savings. Solomon wrote, "The rich man's wealth is his fortress; the ruin of the poor is their poverty" (Proverbs 10:15).

d. To provide for unexpected ministry needs—When we think about financial stewardship, most of us usually think about giving from our weekly income to the church. Certainly that is a biblical concept. But our stewardship responsibilities do not stop there. God's Word also teaches that we should set aside a portion of our income to meet unexpected ministry needs that might arise. Many of us use 1 Corinthians 16:2 as a proof text for tithing to the church. It is emblazoned on our church's offering envelopes.

Yet look carefully at what Paul writes: "On the first day of every week let each one of you put aside and *save*, as he may prosper, that no collections be made when I come" (1 Corinthians 16:2, emphasis mine). Paul instructed the Corinthians to set aside a portion of their income, above their regular giving, for a special ministry need—to feed hungry believers in Jerusalem.

In the same way, I believe we should have a special savings account for funding unexpected needs that might arise in others' lives or in the church. A friend of mine has a bank account into which he contributes 5 percent of his income each month. This is in addition to the tithe he gives to his local church. He calls this his "ministry account," and he uses it to fund a variety of ministry needs: missionary support, financial assistance to others, special needs within the church, and so on. When he has depleted the account, he says no with a clear conscience to any requests for funds until he has replenished the account.

Do you have enough money set aside so that you can freely respond to special ministry needs? I believe that God intends Christians to regularly consume less income than they generate so that they might use their surplus to further God's work.

3. Money is to be accumulated without being trusted

"Two weeks ago you quoted Matthew 6:7 and said that God is not impressed by lengthy prayers. This week you quoted Colossians 4:12 and said that we are to agonize in prayer. Which is it?" Church members quickly notice inconsistencies. So do readers. Nevertheless, truth is often held in tension. Most principles taught in the Bible have corresponding balancing principles. And this is true about saving money. Yes, the Bible teaches that "a rich man's wealth is his fortress." But notice what else the Bible teaches: "The wealth of the rich is their fortified city; they *imagine* it an unscalable wall" (Proverbs 18:11, NIV, emphasis mine). The operative word is *imagine*.

My grandfather had frugally saved money all his life, and he was quite proud of the assets he had accumulated. But one day he was served with a notice: A former business partner was suing him for $35 million. My grandfather's net worth didn't amount to even a fraction of that figure. He suddenly realized that his wealth was not near the protection he had imagined it to be.

No savings account can protect you from *every* adversity in life. Regardless of how much money you stash away, you can easily lose it through a lawsuit, an extended illness, a bad investment, or a prolonged period of unemployment.

Unfortunately, the prodigal son didn't understand the severe limitations of money. And his lack of understanding was the primary drive that led him away from his father and into a prolonged period of bitter disappointment.

Maybe the same thing has happened to you. Your genuine need and responsibility to provide for the material needs of your family has subtly, but definitely, shifted your affection from your Father. You regularly find yourself thinking either about money or the things that money can purchase. You worry about having enough money for your retirement or your children's education. You wonder how you'd survive if you lost your job or became disabled. How can you keep from allowing money to become the focus of your life?

There are no simple answers, no "three easy steps" to make money your slave, rather than your master. Instead, we need to realize that we will always struggle with this age-old temptation to worship the gifts rather than the Giver of those gifts. Perhaps those of us prone to overestimate the importance of money should always have the following prayer on our lips:

> Father, forgive me for allowing material things to become a focus of my life. I pray that You would give me the discipline to save for the future, but the faith to share when I see a need. Help me to understand that no matter how much I have, it will never be enough to protect me from Your anger or discipline. And most of all, remind me that You are the Source of every good thing in my life. Amen.

Two of my closest friends read the last two chapters with completely different reactions. One said, "Robert, you are right on target. I think about money all the time, and it has been a real detriment to my spiritual life."

However, another friend offered a different assessment. He said, "Who are you writing to? Money is no problem in my life. I hardly ever think about it." At first I was somewhat shaken by his statement, until I probed a little further. Although my friend rarely thought about money itself, he frequently conversed and daydreamed about the things money could purchase: cars, vacations, golf clubs, and clothes. Without even realizing it, my friend has become addicted to pleasure.

....

CHAPTER 5

Addicted to Pleasure

How to know if the "good life" is ruining you

In 549 B.C. the Persian king Cyrus had one goal in life: to capture the influential city of Sardis in Asia Minor. Yet the king faced one formidable barrier. Sardis was built on a fifteen-hundred-foot plateau surrounded by steep cliffs impossible to scale. You can understand, then, why the residents of Sardis didn't lie awake at night worrying about enemy invasions. All was secure. Nevertheless, no one understood the intensity of Cyrus's resolve to conquer the city. The king offered a great reward to any of his soldiers who could determine how to penetrate the fortress.

A solider named Hyeroeades accepted the challenge. One day as Hyeroeades stood at the base of the plateau and observed the Sardian soldiers standing guard on top of the city wall, he saw one of the soldiers accidentally drop his helmet over it. Hyeroeades carefully observed the route the soldier took to descend the steep cliff, retrieve his helmet, and return to his place on the wall. That night, while the city slept, Hyeroeades led a garrison of soldiers up the same cliff, over the wall, and into the unguarded city. The city of Sardis was conquered that night for two reasons: The citizens overestimated their immunity from attack and underestimated their enemy's resolve to defeat them.

Unfortunately, too many of us experience defeat in our spiritual lives for exactly those same reasons. First, we overestimate our safety from Satan's attack in our lives. We think that because we've experienced God's saving grace, are members of an evangelical church, have sat under wonderful Bible teaching, and/or have experienced God's supernatural working in our lives, we're immune to spiritual danger. Yet, God's Word says just the opposite. It is God's *children,* not His *enemies,* who are in danger of Satan's conquest. Paul warned the Christians at Corinth about the danger of spiritual complacency: "Therefore let him who thinks he stands take heed lest he fall" (1 Corinthians 10:12).

That word *therefore* should send every reader back to the preceding paragraphs to answer the question, What is that *therefore* there for? Paul had just recounted how God's chosen people, the Israelites, had fallen away from God. Even though they had experienced God's supernatural deliverance from Egypt, His supernatural revelation at Sinai, and His supernatural provision in the wilderness, Paul writes (in one of the great understatements of the New Testament), "Nevertheless, with most of them God was not well pleased; for they were laid low in the wilderness" (1 Corinthians 10:5).

Paul refers here to the hundreds of thousands of Israelites who were prohibited from entering the Promised Land and died in the wilderness because of their sins. Their bodies were "laid low" or, literally, "strewn in the wilderness."

Recently an airliner carrying 134 passengers crashed a few minutes after takeoff. News footage shot from a helicopter flying over the crash site showed wreckage, luggage, and body parts strewn over several miles. It was a gruesome reminder of the danger of flying. Paul uses similar imagery in 1 Corinthians 10:5. If you had flown over the Palestinian desert during Moses' time, you'd have seen countless Israelite bodies rotting in the wilderness because of their rebellion against God. Why? They had mistakenly assumed that because God had blessed them in the past, they could ignore His demands for the present. Those people, once labeled "God's chosen," became lifeless corpses in the desert, a gruesome reminder of the danger of complacency.

Against that historical backdrop Paul warned the Corinthians, as well as all of us today, about overestimating our safety from enemy attack. "Therefore let him who thinks he stands take heed lest he fall." No matter what mountaintop spiritual experiences we've enjoyed in the past, we should never overestimate our safety from greed, lust, or rebellion against God.

But an equally fatal mistake in spiritual warfare is to underestimate the Enemy's resolve to destroy us. As we saw in chapter 2, Satan has a scheme—a blueprint—for our destruction. He is intent on destroying our marriages, our children, our peace of mind, and our relationships with God. And this last relationship is the focus of this book.

How does Satan destroy a Christian's relationship with his or her Heavenly Father? Subtly. Very subtly. I like the way my former professor Haddon Robinson puts it: "When Satan comes to you, he does not come in the form of a coiled snake. He does not approach with the roar of a lion. He does not come with the wail of a siren. He does not come waving a red flag. Satan simply slides into your life. When he appears, he seems almost like a comfortable companion. There's nothing about him that you would dread."[1]

As the character Mephistopheles says in Shakespeare's *Faust*, "The people do not know the devil is there even when he has them by the throat."

How does Satan slip into your life, grab you by the throat, and choke your love for your Heavenly Father? What does Satan's blueprint for your destruction look like? Actually, Satan isn't very original; he doesn't have to be. For thousands of years he has ensnared people with the same three traps we've been discussing in this book: money, pleasure, and ambition. In the last two chapters we've seen how a preoccupation with money can lead us from God. In this chapter, we'll explore how pleasure can become an equally potent force in captivating the heart of a Christian.

THE BIBLICAL VIEW OF PLEASURE

Is there something wrong with choosing to watch a television program instead of praying, or flipping through your favorite catalogue instead of turning the pages of your Bible, or daydreaming about your next vacation instead of the wonders of heaven?

We Christians tend to go to one of two extremes in our attitude toward pleasure. One of those extremes is a hyperintensive program of self-discipline, denying ourselves the normal pleasures of everyday life. Sickened by our lack of self-control, our weight, our slothfulness, or our inconsistency in Bible study and prayer, we decide to "deny ourselves." We cut out desserts, we quit watching television, we refuse to buy new clothes, and we trade our plans for the Carnival cruise for a mission trip in Haiti.

That program lasts for several _____ (fill in the blank: months, days, hours, minutes), then we fall into the same rut. No, scratch that. Not the *same* rut, but a *deeper* rut. We feel so discouraged about our lack of self-control that we give up completely trying to live any kind of a disciplined life. There *has* to be a better way.

There is. To get a handle on this subject of pleasure, we need to understand what God's Word says—and doesn't say—about this topic. Contrary to some observers' stereotype of Christianity, God never meant for us to completely deprive ourselves of enjoyment. Lewis Sperry Chafer correctly asserts that: "Spirituality is not a pious pose. It is not a 'Thou shalt not'; it is 'Thou shalt.' It flings open the doors into the eternal blessedness, energies and resources of God. It is a serious thing to remove the element of relaxation and play from any life. We cannot be normal physically, mentally or spiritually if we neglect this vital factor in human life. God has provided that our joy shall be full."[2]

We need to remember that God did not only endow us with a spirit, but also with a body. With that body comes the need for food, sex, exercise, and relaxation. In my book *Guilt-Free Living,* I devote an entire chapter to the subject of "Guilt-Free Relaxation." Without repeating the material in that book, let me direct your attention to two important Bible verses that give us God's perspective about pleasure. We find both verses in the Book of Ecclesiastes written by King Solomon, the wisest man who ever lived. Most scholars believe that Solomon wrote Ecclesiastes later in life. Some people wrongly assume that because Solomon wandered from God for a prolonged period of time, we must interpret Ecclesiastes as *earthly* instead of *heavenly* wisdom. I disagree. I think that Solomon's varied experiences gave him a unique, refreshing, and balanced view of life and of pleasure.

Let me illustrate what I mean. If the doctor told you that you have only twenty-four hours to live, what would you do? After the shock wore off, how would you spend your last day on this planet? Some would say that the *right* answer is read your Bible, pray, witness, cash in your CDs, and give everything to the church.

But Solomon offers a different perspective. He spends the first six verses of Ecclesiastes 9 speaking of death's inevitability. Like the animals, we're all going to die. So what does the world's wisest man say we should do? Contrary to what we might think is the *spiritual* answer, Solomon advises, "Go then, eat your bread in happiness, and drink your wine with a cheerful heart; for God has already approved your works" (Ecclesiastes 9:7).

The fact that the ticking clock moves us closer and closer to our departure from this planet doesn't mean we should deny ourselves pleasure in life. God wants us to enjoy the brief life he has given us, not just endure it.

"But doesn't the Bible teach that we are created to work? Didn't Solomon himself write, 'Poor is he who works with a negligent hand, but the hand of the diligent makes rich'"? Yes, there is a time for work, but there is also a time for pleasure and relaxation. Solomon also wrote, "For what does a man get in all his labor and in his striving with which he labors under the sun? Because all his days his task is painful and grievous; even at night his mind does not rest. This too is vanity. There is nothing better for a man than to eat and drink and tell himself that his labor is good. This also I have seen, that it is from the hand of God" (Ecclesiastes 2:22–24).

God has wired each of us in such a way that we cannot work twelve hours a day, seven days a week, fifty-two weeks each year. God's Word says that there's more to life than work and religious duty. Pleasure has a place in our lives.

THE DANGERS OF PLEASURE

However, God's Word also clearly sounds some warnings about pleasure (emphases mine):

He who loves *pleasure* will become a poor man. (Proverbs 21:17)

And the seed which fell among the thorns, these are the ones who have heard, and as they go on their way they are choked with worries and riches and *pleasures* of this life, and bring no fruit to maturity. (Luke 8:14)

For men will be lovers of self, lovers of money, boastful, arrogant, revilers, disobedient to parents, ungrateful, unholy...lovers of *pleasure* rather than lovers of God. (2 Timothy 3:2, 4)

You have lived luxuriously on the earth and led a life of wanton *pleasure;* you have fattened your hearts in a day of slaughter. (James 5:5)

The above passages explain that pleasure, like money, is neither moral nor immoral in itself. But pleasure is wrong in specific circumstances. Specifically, pleasure leads us away from God when...

It is in excess

Recently I've been under a lot of pressure at work, so I decided to treat myself and my family to twenty-four hours of hedonism. On a Friday afternoon, we packed the car, drove to Dallas, and stayed at a luxury hotel in one of the most upscale malls in the country. We abandoned our diets and had a sumptuous dinner of sour-cream enchiladas; strolled into our favorite stores to purchase some fun, but not necessary, clothes; and enjoyed a midnight movie. After sleeping late the next morning, we shopped some more, enjoyed another movie, ate another meal at a favorite restaurant, and drove home.

"What's wrong with that?" you ask. Nothing, really. Except when the *next* Friday afternoon rolled around, I wanted to do the same thing. Although neither my checkbook nor my schedule would allow it, I desperately wanted to relive the pleasures of that weekend. Perhaps you've had a similar experience. You read one novel just for fun, then decide to read another. One television program quickly evolves into an entire evening of viewing. One scoop of ice cream causes you to crave another. Two weeks of vacation make you long for an entire month. Pleasure can become addictive! I believe the biblical writers warn us of this addictive nature of pleasure when they caution us against becoming *lovers* of it.

There's nothing wrong with relaxation, even an occasional indulgence, as long as we keep it in balance. The Bible outlines an appropriate formula for work and relaxation: "Six days you shall labor and do all your work, but the seventh day is a sabbath of the LORD our God; in it you shall not do any work" (Exodus 20:9–10). Too many religionists have twisted the sabbath into a day of inconsistent restrictions instead of understanding its original purpose. ("Thou shalt not go to the movies, but thou mayest watch football on thy television.") Jesus said that this day of rest is for man's benefit, not God's (Mark 2:27). It is a day to recharge our physical, emotional, and spiritual batteries. God made us in such a way that we need weekly breaks from our work and a time to think about spiritual matters. And so He established a clear work/rest pattern: work, work, work, work, work, work, *rest*, work, work, work, work, work, work, *rest*…

Notice the pattern is not work, work, *rest, rest, rest*, work, *rest* as some would like. Also notice that the Bible sets no precedent for working yourself nonstop for forty years so you can spend the last fifteen to twenty years of your life doing no work at all. Although retirement is a popular idea in our culture, it isn't part of God's plan. God never intended for us to spend the final years or decades of our lives with no greater purpose than deciding where to park our Winnebago or with whom we should play golf tomorrow.

I think of one couple I know in their midfifties who decided to retire early. Up until their retirement they directed a junior high school Sunday school department and enthusiastically witnessed for Christ. But retirement changed all that. Their retirement "schedule" keeps them from participating in any church ministry. In fact, they rarely attend church these days. In my few conversations with them recently, I've discerned that they no longer have the zeal for God they once had. They've become "lovers of pleasure" because they don't really understand God's balance between work and rest.

Am I saying that a person must work at his job until he dies? No. But even if you retire from your vocation, you can perform many other useful services in your church, civic organization, or local hospital. You can fulfill a meaningful purpose with the abundance of time you now have.

Following God's pattern for work and relaxation can keep us from excessively indulging in pleasure.

Pleasure is also wrong when…

It becomes our life-focus

Let me ask you three simple questions to help you determine your focus in life:

1. What do you talk about most often?
2. What do you think about most often?
3. If someone were to give you a check for twenty thousand dollars, how would you spend it?

Your answers to those questions reveal your priorities. If vacations, hobbies, recreational pursuits, sensuality, or comfort dominate your answers to the above questions, pleasure is probably your life-focus. In fact, pleasure may have become your idol. We make a grave mistake when we limit idols to wooden or silver statues. An idol is any person or thing we love more than God. And whatever we talk about, think about, and spend our hard-earned money for defines what we really love. The apostle Peter explained it this way: "For by what a man is overcome, by this he is enslaved" (2 Peter 2:19).

Some years ago I prepared a series of messages on Colossians 3 which encourages us to "set [our] minds on the things above, not on the things that are on earth" (v. 2). One book I studied during my preparation challenged me to ask this question: "What are the three things that I think about the most?" As I honestly assessed my thoughts, I was embarrassed at how often I dwelt on things that fall under the heading of pleasure: vacation destinations, restaurants, hobbies to pursue, books to read, and movies. (I confess: I *love* going to the movies.) While none of those activities is inherently wrong, I had allowed them to become the focus of my life. That realization motivated me to make some radical changes in my life.

Have you allowed yourself to be enslaved by pleasure?

Finally, pleasure is wrong when...

It violates God's Word

Up to this point, our discussion of pleasure hasn't included the enjoyment of immoral activities. Obviously adultery, homosexuality, and premarital sex clearly violate the Bible's teaching and hinder our relationship with God. We all understand how those sins lead us from our Heavenly Father.

Yet we also need to recognize the relationship between sexual immorality and other types of pleasure. I believe that people who allow themselves to become *lovers* of pleasure—I'm referring to movies, malls, and sour-cream enchiladas—can easily become entangled in sexual sin. We see that truth illustrated in the prodigal son's life.

Luke 15 tells us that the prodigal son spent all his money on "loose living." When we speak of someone who lives *loosely,* we think of sexual immorality, but that isn't what the Greek word means in this verse. Greek literature uses this word to describe "wasteful and extravagant living." James has the same thought in mind when he writes, "You have lived luxuriously on earth and led a life of wanton (or wasteful) pleasure" (James 5:5). I came across a vivid description of this kind of lifestyle in a book about the famous motion picture director George Cukor:

He was lying between French silk sheets in a British Regency bed drinking bitter Parisian coffee and reading the *New York Times*. Fluttering about him was a covey of domestics who catered to his every whim. Cukor's valet stood near the bed with a pad as Cukor dictated his preferences for lunch. Minutes later, the kitchen was abuzz as the cooks prepared finger sandwiches, one small slice of pâté and tiny silver bowls of Nicosia salad. Soon the meal would be packed in a wicker hamper and deposited in the backseat of a Rolls Royce. His valet was equally busy, setting out a linen shirt, a pair of Savile Row slacks and Italian leather shoes. Finally, Cukor aroused himself from his regal boudoir, ordered the Rolls Royce and began his hated trip to the studio.[3]

Tired of the discipline and restrictions imposed by a father who had probably earned his wealth through hard labor, the prodigal son was ready to enjoy his wealth and live the kind of life described above. Who could blame him? However, his lack of self-control not only led to poverty but also to immorality. Later, the older brother reveals the other indulgences his younger brother enjoyed: "But when this son of yours came, who has devoured your wealth with harlots, you killed the fattened calf for him" (Luke 15:30).

We see the same relationship between pleasure and immorality in David's life. Although King David was a man after God's heart, the victor over Goliath, and the most successful of Israel's kings, we mainly remember him for his one night of passion with Bathsheba. This mistake marked both him and his family forever. What caused such a great man to fall into adultery and murder? I believe that David had become a lover of pleasure. As king over Israel, he became accustomed to an easy life. Just look at 2 Samuel 11:1. "Then it happened in the spring, at the time when kings go out to battle, that David sent Joab and his servants with him and all Israel, and they destroyed the sons of Ammon and besieged Rabbah. But David stayed at Jerusalem."

In those days, kings led their men into battle. But David chose to stay home. David knew he should have been with his men. He probably felt guilty for remaining in the palace. But he couldn't make himself go. He was tired of lugging his heavy armor around the hot Palestinian desert. He had paid his dues as a young soldier; he could let someone else do the work. The king deserved *some* luxuries.

David's inability to make his desires subservient to his will caused him other problems that night. Seeing Bathsheba, the wife of one of his men, bathing on the roof next door, David could not harness his longings. "And David sent messengers and took her, and when she came to him, he lay with her; and when she had purified herself from her uncleanness, she returned to her house" (2 Samuel 11:4).

David never had much self-discipline. We see David's inability to control his sensual appetite throughout his reign. When anointed king at age eighteen, David was a single man. By the time he actually assumed the throne, he had taken six wives in direct violation of God's law prohibiting multiple wives for kings. The scholar F. B. Meyer sums up how David's desire for pleasure finally led to his downfall: "In direct violation of the law of Moses, he took more concubines and wives; fostering in him a habit of sensual indulgence, which predisposed him to the evil invitation of that evening hour."[4]

A strong relationship exists between our ability to curb our desire for pleasure and our ability to avoid immorality. Perhaps the late poet and dramatist Oscar Wilde expresses that relationship most eloquently when he writes about his own life:

> The gods have given me almost everything, but I let myself be lured into long spells of senseless and sensual ease. Tired of being on the heights, I deliberately went to the depths in search of a new sensation. What paradox was to me in the sphere of thought, perversity became to me in the sphere of passion. I grew careless of the lives of other people. I took pleasure where it pleased me, and passed on. And I forgot that every little action of the common day makes or

unmakes character. And that therefore, what one has done in the secret chamber, one has some day to cry aloud from the housetop. I ceased to be lord over myself. I was no longer the captain of my soul, and I did not know it. I allowed pleasure to dominate me, and I ended in horrible disgrace.[5]

How can we keep from allowing pleasure to dominate our lives and eclipse our relationships with God?

....

CHAPTER 6

Lessons from the Pentathlon

Learning to balance pleasure with discipline

A young mother once approached Confederate General Robert E. Lee with her baby, wanting the famed general to bless her son. Lee took the infant in his arms and then, looking at the mother, said, "Teach him he must deny himself." What a strange thing to say to a young mother and infant! But General Lee understood what the masses fail to comprehend: Discipline is the key to success in every area of life including our relationships with God.

Unfortunately, the prodigal son never learned that "he must deny himself." The promise of pleasure in that distant land caused him to pack his bags and leave his father.

Perhaps, as I did a number of years ago, you've allowed pleasure to dominate your thoughts and suffocate your relationship with God. Or maybe you want to make sure that such a thing never happens to you. How can you keep yourself from becoming addicted to pleasure?

I encourage you to change into something comfortable, put on some running shoes, and allow the apostle Paul to become your own personal trainer for the next few moments.

RUNNING TO WIN

The apostle Paul understood the importance of refusing to allow pleasure to rule his life. He realized that the inability to control both his natural and sinful desires could have disastrous consequences in his relationship with God. In fact, Paul had an overwhelming concern that a lapse in self-control would one day ruin his life and ministry, and more importantly, damage the reputation of Jesus Christ. Thus, Paul continually battled with discipline and self-control in his life: "I buffet my body and make it my slave, lest possibly, after I have preached to others, I myself should be disqualified" (1 Corinthians 9:27).

What does Paul mean by "I buffet my body"? To fully appreciate his imagery, one needs to read the entire paragraph:

> Do you not know that those who run in a race all run, but only one receives the prize? Run in such a way that you may win. And everyone who competes in the games exercises self-control in all things. They then do it to receive a perishable wreath, but we an imperishable. Therefore I run in such a way, as not without aim; I box in such a way, as not beating the air; but I buffet my body and make it my slave, lest possibly, after I have preached to others, I myself should be disqualified. (1 Corinthians 9:24–27)

If you read between the lines of Paul's writings, you'll conclude that he was a sports enthusiast. He uses many metaphors from the athletic realm to describe the Christian life. For example, he describes the Christian life as a wrestling match in Ephesians 6:12 and as a boxing tournament in 1 Corinthians 9:26. But his favorite metaphor for the Christian life is a footrace. Paul says that a competitor in a footrace has one goal in mind: to win. It isn't enough just to be in the competition; a runner must have an insatiable desire to win. And that strong desire to win translates into some specific steps of action.

For just a moment, let's consider Paul's command to "run in such a way as to win." Paul says that if we desire to win in the Christian life and receive rewards at the judgment seat of Christ, we must commit ourselves to the same discipline a runner commits himself to in order to win a race. How do we cultivate that kind of discipline? By adopting four actions, all of which involve breaking our addiction to pleasure.

1. Remove any excess "weight"

A runner doesn't carry any excess pounds if he or she is intent on winning the race. When is the last time you saw an obese person crossing the finish line? Can you ever recall seeing a relay runner dressed in a wool suit or overcoat? Of course not. Runners know that to win they must travel as lightly as possible.

The writer of Hebrews (who also must have been a sports enthusiast) wrote: "Therefore, since we have so great a cloud of witnesses surrounding us, let us also lay aside every encumbrance, and the sin which so easily entangles us, and let us run with endurance the race that is set before us" (Hebrews 12:1).

The author of Hebrews identifies the excess weight we need to shed: sin. Wrong attitudes, actions, or thoughts will weigh you down in your Christian life and cause you to lose both the race and ultimately your reward. To win in the Christian life, you must decisively deal with sin *now*. Pause for a moment and ask yourself the following questions:

- Are you entangled in relationships that you know displease the Lord?
- Are secret habits constantly dragging you down in your spiritual life?
- Are wrong attitudes, such as bitterness or a critical spirit, poisoning you?

Those who are addicted to pleasure find it easy to rationalize detrimental relationships, habits, and attitudes. Eliminating them involves too much pain, and the pleasure addict finds it difficult to willingly endure discomfort. But if you want to regain control over your spiritual life, you have to lay aside those wrong relationships, actions, and attitudes.

Some people respond by saying, "I'm not strong enough to lay aside those things on my own. I'm going to pray and let God take responsibility for removing those sins from my life." If you adopt this attitude, I guarantee you will fail, and fail miserably. Why? Consider two important truths from Scripture:

(1) You are responsible for laying aside sin. Hebrews 12:1 says "let *us* also lay aside." God says it's *your* responsibility, not His, to remove sin from your life. Perhaps you're familiar with the management term *upward delegation.* In the past I've had some staff members who were experts in upward delegation. I'd ask them to write a letter, make a phone call, or oversee a project. A few days later they'd say to me, "Pastor, I don't know how to do this. Would you mind doing it instead?" That is upward delegation.

We cannot upwardly delegate to God something He has commanded us to do. God isn't responsible for removing sin from my life. I am!

(2) You are capable of removing sin from your life. God never asks us to do something He hasn't empowered us to do. Romans 6:4–6 reminds us that God has already given us the power to remove sin from our lives: "Therefore we have been buried with Him through baptism into death, in order that as Christ was raised from the dead through the glory of the Father, so we too might walk in newness of life. For if we have become united with Him in the likeness of His death, certainly we shall be also in the likeness of His resurrection, knowing this, that our old self was crucified with Him, that our body of sin might be done away with, that we should no longer be slaves to sin."

When you become a Christian, the same power that raised Jesus Christ from the grave operates in your life to give you power over sin. Sin has no more power over your life than you choose to allow it to have. Remember the story of the ten-ton elephant tied down by the small stake?

Many Christians allow sin to weigh them down because they don't understand the tremendous power available to them. Many of us live as slaves to our wrong actions, attitudes, and relationships. But God's Word says we have already received the power necessary to lay aside sin in our lives.

2. Say no to a specific pleasure every day

Paul says in 1 Corinthians 9:27 that he would constantly "buffet his body"—literally, he beat it black and blue—to make his body his slave. An athlete determined to win the race must discipline him- or herself. The athlete must make a slave *of* desire instead of remaining a slave *to* desire.

John MacArthur Jr. provides us with some great insight into Paul's statement:

> Most people, including many Christians, are instead slaves to their bodies. Their bodies tell their minds what to do. Their bodies decide when to eat, what to eat, how much to eat, when to sleep and get up, and so on. An athlete cannot allow that. He follows the training rules, not his body. He runs when he would rather be resting, he eats a balanced meal when he would rather have a chocolate sundae, he goes to bed when he would rather stay up, and he gets up early to train when he would rather stay in bed. An athlete leads his body; he does not follow it. It is his slave, not the other way around.[1]

All of us have a tendency to allow pleasure to dominate our lives. That's why we must regularly practice self-discipline. Dr. Howard Hendricks used to exhort our seminary class to "Say no to at least one thing in your life every day, just to remind your body who is in charge." What great advice!

Make it a daily practice to refuse something from which you derive pleasure—a piece of pie, an extra hour in the sack, a television program—not because there's anything sinful about that pleasure, but because you need to practice maintaining control over your desires. Saint Francis used to refer to the human body as "Brother Ass" (Perhaps *donkey* would be more appropriate in a Christian book!) because we are to ride the donkey instead of allowing the donkey to ride us. By saying no to something pleasurable every day, we can remain in control!

3. Allocate your energy wisely

In Paul's day, an athlete didn't have the luxury of excelling in only one sport; instead, he had to train for several events. The most popular Greek contest was the pentathlon which involved a footrace, the discus throw, wrestling, the javelin throw, and the long jump. This explains why Paul mentions two sports, running and boxing, in 1 Corinthians 9:24–27. He says, "everyone who competes in the games exercises self-control in *all* things" (v. 25, emphasis mine). If an athlete hoped to win the victor's crown at the end of the competition, he had to exhibit proficiency in many areas, not just one. Thus the athlete had to wisely allocate his training time to cover all areas in which he would compete.

The same truth applies to the Christian life. When we have one life-area under control, we often think we can sit back and relax. But the person who wants to win in the Christian life doesn't have the luxury of concentrating on only one life-area. To avoid allowing pleasure to derail our lives, we must learn to wisely allocate our time and energy among the various responsibilities God has given us.

What are those responsibilities? Certainly our overriding assignment is to help fulfill the Great Commission by making Christian disciples of all people. This is our greatest responsibility, but not our *only* responsibility. We're also responsible for our families, our jobs, our financial affairs, our health, our friendships, and a number of other areas. If we want to win both in this life and at the judgment seat of Christ, we must give attention to all these areas.

We all know of people who devote too much time to their work, neglecting their families. We say such people are unbalanced. But a person who devotes all his or her time and energy to family, neglecting his or her spiritual life or friendships, is *also* unbalanced. If we want to run to win, we must give appropriate attention to all the life-areas over which God holds us accountable.

How can you keep from being overwhelmed by these various and sometimes competing responsibilities? Last week, I spent about forty-five minutes in an exercise that you might find helpful. On a legal-sized sheet of paper, I listed seven life-areas that are important to me and, I believe, to God: spiritual health, physical health, vocation, family, finances, social interaction, and personal growth. Beside each life-area, I wrote down one goal I hope to attain within the next six months. Let me show you what part of that sheet looked like:

- Spiritual health: Set alarm clock fifteen minutes earlier beginning tomorrow morning in order to read one chapter from Proverbs each day.
- Physical health: Eat one apple and one banana each day beginning today.
- Family: Have one "date" with Amy each week beginning this Thursday night.
- Finances: Set up a mutual fund account for Julia's college fund, and begin depositing $150 into that account each month beginning this month.

Will reading one chapter of Proverbs a day take care of *all* my spiritual needs? Is eating two pieces of fruit daily *everything* I need to do to maintain good health? Is taking my wife on a date once a week the *only* thing I need to do to improve my family life? Of course not. I could create an unending list of goals for each life-area! In fact, in the past I've filled entire tablets with goals for those seven life-areas. And that's where my goals remained—on the list. I never translated them into action because I felt so overwhelmed. I've discovered that I enhance successful living when I concentrate on one short-term goal for each major life-area. This allows me to focus my energies on the things I deem important.

Setting obtainable goals is such a simple principle for successful living, yet few take advantage of it. Research has demonstrated that only 3 percent of Americans have clearly defined goals in life. This is a shame, because the old adage is really true: Aim at nothing and you'll hit it every time. Lest you think I'm merely spouting a lot of positive-thinking rhetoric, consider Paul's words in 1 Corinthians 9:26: "Therefore I run in such a way, as not without aim; I box in such a way, as not beating the air." Paul knew that to win in this life and in the life to come, he had to have clearly defined goals.

4. Keep your eye on the finish line

A runner who allows the weather, spectators in the stands, or other runners to distract him or her will eventually stumble. If a runner really wants to win, he must keep his thoughts on making it across the finish line. A winner runs the race with the end in mind.

In the same way, we must live our lives with the end clearly in focus. And the end is not graduation, marriage, the presidency of our company, or retirement. Our finish line is the judgment seat of Christ. Paul describes it this way: "For we must all appear before the judgment seat of Christ, that each one may be recompensed for his deeds in the body according to what he has done, whether good or bad" (2 Corinthians 5:10).

One writer says that we need to develop a "bema mentality." Bema is the Greek term for the judgment seat of Christ. To have a "bema mentality" means that we constantly evaluate every word, thought, action, and attitude based on how Jesus Christ will one day judge it. The strongest motivation for breaking our natural addiction to pleasure is realizing that one day the trumpet will sound and our holy God will summon us to account for the ways we've spent our lives.

Joe Wall tells the story about a duck who broke his wing during his flight south for the winter. A sympathetic farmer retrieved the fallen duck and took him home. The farmer's children adopted the duck as their pet, feeding him from the table and taking him along as they performed their daily chores. The next fall, the children were heartbroken as they watched the duck struggle to join the other ducks who were flying south for the winter. But the duck's wing wasn't strong enough for the flight. Every time a flock flew overhead, the duck looked longingly into the sky then returned to play with the children.

The second year the duck's wing had grown much stronger. But the children had fed him so well that when he attempted to take off, he was too fat to get off the ground. After one or two attempts, he gave up and returned to play with the children.

The third year, the duck was completely healed. But as the other ducks quacked their call to go south, the duck never even looked up as they flew over. He had become accustomed to the comfort of his new existence, losing his focus on the true calling of his life.[2]

We can easily fall into the "fat duck" mentality. If we don't watch ourselves, pleasure and comfort can subtly but quickly become our life's focus. Remember that the prodigal son allowed pleasure to entice him from his father and temporarily blind him to his ultimate purpose. But if we want to run to win, we have to keep our eyes fixed on our final destination, always longing and constantly disciplining ourselves for that final day when we will fly away to meet our Lord.

Perhaps as you've read this chapter you've determined a course of action that will help you avoid the pitfalls of pleasure-seeking. Maybe you've resolved to enhance discipline in your life so that you can run the race to win. I commend you for your resolve. However, you need to know something. Discipline and goal setting can draw you *to* your Heavenly Father, but it also can actually lead you *further* from Him when you pursue them for the wrong reasons. What do I mean? You'll see in the next chapter.

....

Declarations of Independence

How Satan turns healthy ambition into unhealthy independence

The morning after the great Chicago fire of 1871 destroyed the city, a group of the city's leading merchants stood on State Street surveying the remains of the great stores they had built. After assessing the damage, they adjourned to a conference room to discuss their future. Should they remain in the city and try to rebuild their stores, or would they profit more by moving to another part of the country? Given the desolation of the city, it really wasn't a difficult decision. All of the store owners decided to relocate except one, Marshall Field. Pointing to the smoldering remains of his store, Field said, "Gentlemen, on that very spot I will build the world's greatest store, no matter how many times it burns down." Motivational writer Napoleon Hill writes,

> The store was built. It stands there today, a towering monument to the power of that state of mind known as a burning desire. The easy thing for Marshall Field to have done would have been exactly what his fellow merchants did. When the going was hard, and the future looked dismal, they pulled up and went where the going seemed easier. Wishing will not bring riches. But desiring riches with a state of mind that becomes an obsession, then planning definite ways and

means to acquire riches, and backing those plans with persistence which does not recognize failure, will bring riches.[1]

Goals, desire, determination, persistence—we've all been taught to appreciate these words. Our history abounds with examples of men and women who have succeeded in life because of dogged determination. I think of a ten-year-old boy and his friend who accidentally poured gasoline instead of kerosene on a stove fire in a small country schoolhouse. The explosion killed the friend immediately and injured the ten-year-old so severely that the doctors were certain they'd have to amputate both his legs. However, the boy's parents asked the doctors to delay the amputation. "Give us just one more day," they pleaded. Each day the boy's parents begged for just a little more time. Eventually the boy's legs healed, although when the doctors removed the bandages, the child's left leg was two and one-half inches shorter than his right. His right foot was missing most of its toes.

The doctors said, "The boy will never walk again." But through persistence, he walked. "The boy will never walk without crutches," the doctors said. But with great determination, he walked without crutches.

The young boy then began to jog and finally to run. Within a few years, Glen Cunningham had become an Olympic star and earned the title "the world's fastest human being."[2]

Whenever I speak on the topic of perseverance, I like to remind people that it took Thomas Edison eighteen hundred attempts to invent the electric light bulb. Babe Ruth struck out 1,330 times, yet we consider him one of America's greatest ballplayers. George Bernard Shaw received rejection notices for his first five novels.

And what about Ludwig van Beethoven? Most of us know something of Beethoven's great successes: his nine symphonies, five concertos, and beautiful chamber music. But many of us forget the tremendous handicap he had to overcome. While in his twenties, Beethoven began to lose his hearing. By the time he was fifty, he was stone deaf. At one point, Beethoven's handicap so frustrated him that he slammed both fists on his keyboard and yelled, "I will take life by the throat!" Beethoven knew that the key to his success would be determination and perseverance in spite of his circumstances.[3]

We admire people who know what they want in life and will do whatever necessary to achieve their goals. But there's also a dark side to ambition. Sometimes our thirst for success can actually lead us *away* from our Heavenly Father. We have to learn how to maintain the delicate balance between good stewardship of our God-given abilities and selfish ambition that leads to a life of independence.

We've already identified two desires that subtly lead us from our Father just as the prodigal son was lured from his father: money and pleasure. Now we come to the third desire that caused the prodigal son, and causes us, to leave home: ambition. The prodigal son grew tired of living in his father's and older brother's shadows. The clock was ticking. He felt his life slowly slipping away. If he was ever going to make his mark on the world, he had to cut his family ties. So the son left home, not in the normal leaving and cleaving process described in Genesis 2:24–25, but in an act of outright rebellion against his father's authority.

I should stop here and point out that nothing is inherently wrong with wanting to achieve something significant in life. I believe that God has given each one of us a unique purpose in life and a strong desire to achieve that purpose. Many times that strong desire is tied to our biological clocks. A management-consultant friend of mine says that the average age most entrepreneurs begin their new businesses is thirty-nine. Is this a random age for such a choice? My friend doesn't think so. When we reach the midlife years and realize that we have more years behind us than ahead of us, we're willing to take risks to make our mark on the world. For some that risk involves starting new businesses.

Ambition in and of itself is not necessarily sinful anymore than money or pleasure are inherently sinful. However, Satan can take our natural, God-given ambition and use it to gradually turn our hearts from God. Our Enemy is a master at it. In fact, Satan's own ambition drove him from heaven.

A FALLEN STAR

As a spirit being, Satan (originally Lucifer) had little use for money or sensual pleasure, two things he employs to lead us astray. No, Satan's Achilles heel was ambition. His resolve to reach the top of his profession, regardless of the cost, resulted in his downfall.

Two passages in the Old Testament vividly describe how ambition caused God's number one associate to become His number one adversary. First, let's look at Ezekiel 28:

> Son of man, take up a lamentation over the king of Tyre, and say to him, "Thus says the Lord God, 'You had the seal of perfection, full of wisdom and perfect in beauty. You were in Eden, the garden of God; every precious stone was your covering…. You were the anointed cherub who covers, and I placed you there. You were on the holy mountain of God…. You were blameless in your ways from the day you were created, until unrighteousness was found in you. By the abundance of your trade you were internally filled with violence, and you sinned. Therefore I have cast you as profane from the mountain of God. And I have destroyed you, O covering cherub, from the midst of the stones of fire. Your heart was lifted up because of your beauty; you corrupted your wisdom by reason of your splendor.' " (vv. 12–17)

Although God commissioned Ezekiel to deliver this message to the king of Tyre, a very real person in history, He obviously intended this message for someone other than a human being. The king of Tyre did not possess "the seal of perfection" nor was he "full of wisdom and perfect in beauty." Why would Ezekiel refer to him as "the anointed cherub" who was "blameless in your ways from the day you were created"? This passage obviously explains how Lucifer, the chief of God's angelic order, fell from heaven.

God reminded Satan that he had God's approval until the day that "unrighteousness was found in you." What was this "unrighteousness"? Another Old Testament prophet answers that question for us:

"How you have fallen from heaven, O star of the morning, son of the dawn! You have been cut down to the earth, you who have weakened the nations! But you said in your heart, 'I will ascend to heaven; I will raise my throne above the stars of God, and I will sit on the mount of assembly in the recesses of the north. I will ascend above the heights of the clouds; I will make myself like the Most High.'" (Isaiah 14:12–14)

Like Ezekiel, Isaiah had two audiences in mind for his message. His immediate audience was the evil king of Babylon, but his ultimate audience was the power behind that king: Satan. In these verses we find five examples of Satan's unbridled ambition that led to his fall from heaven:

1. *"I will ascend to heaven."* Lucifer had access to the third heaven, God's dwelling place. In fact, as the "anointed cherub," he probably was the worship leader over all the angels. But Satan wanted more than mere access to heaven; he wanted to *rule* over heaven.

2. *"I will raise my throne above the stars of God."* Job 38:7 uses the term *stars* to refer to angels. Although God gave Lucifer responsibility over other angels, he longed for *absolute* authority over the angels.

3. *"I will sit on the mount of the assembly in the recesses of the north."* Pagan literature in Isaiah's day described a council of Babylonian gods that ruled the universe from "the recesses of the north." Thus, Lucifer indicated his desire to rule not only the angels but the entire universe.

4. *"I will ascend above the heights of the clouds."* In the Old Testament, clouds often represented God's glory (Exodus 16:10). In this statement, Lucifer communicated his intent to have a glory that surpassed God's glory.

5. *"I will make myself like the Most High."* Just in case anyone has missed Lucifer's ultimate goal in life, he spells it out clearly here. Although he was a created being who owed his very existence to God, he wanted to supplant God and reign as absolute monarch over the universe.

Satan's declarations sound uncomfortably similar to the mantra of the positive-thinking movement today: "Whatever the mind can conceive and believe, the mind can achieve." What was wrong with Satan's desire? There was nothing sinful about Lucifer wanting to excel in the role God had created for him, just as there's nothing wrong with our desire to succeed. But Satan made a twofold mistake: (1) He wanted absolute control over his own destiny, and (2) he wanted freedom from God's authority. Erwin Lutzer clearly explains the disastrous consequences of Satan's attitude: "Lucifer... sincerely miscalculated both the consequence of his decision and God's reaction to it. He suddenly found himself in a predicament that he could not have foreseen. He thought he was in control of his own future, but it soon became clear that his tomorrows would be determined by the very One whom he had so arrogantly spurned. His supposed lurch into freedom was a plunge into bondage."[4]

Since we've spent the last few pages "in the heavenlies" discussing ancient prophecies that may seem far-removed from your everyday life, let's get practical for a moment. Does the Bible say that all ambition is wrong? Before you answer too quickly, consider a few common scenarios.

A businessman learns through the office grapevine that his supervisor is being kicked upstairs, and he'd like to take his supervisor's place. Why? He has mixed motives. Sure, he'd like the prestige of a new title, and he wouldn't mind having a bigger office either. The larger salary would enable him to perform some much-needed repairs around the house. And maybe he wouldn't have to worry so much about funding his two children's college educations.

What about this situation? A mother decides to go back to school so that she can finish her degree and begin a career in nursing now that her children are teenagers. However, she needs financial assistance to attend school, and five other people have applied for the scholarship she desperately needs. Is she wrong to pursue that scholarship at the expense of the other applicants?

One more example. For ten years, a pastor has struggled in a small church of less than one hundred people. The congregation barely pays him a living wage and, in spite of his diligent sermon preparation and exhaustive personal efforts at visitation, the church hasn't grown. In fact, attendance continues to decline. A fellow minister asks if he'd like to be recommended to a larger church searching for a person with his skills, experience, and dedication. Is it wrong for the pastor to provide a résumé and sermon tape for the church to consider? Is it sinful to desire a larger place of ministry?

In truth, the above situations don't have any inherently *correct* answers. Whether ambition is right or wrong in any situation depends on a variety of factors. As I look through Scripture, I discover three instances when ambition falls into sinfulness. Ambition is wrong when...

1. It becomes the predominant desire of our lives

A well-known politician reached the top of his party through hard work, perseverance, and a singular commitment to his goal. At the age of forty-nine, he moved into the basement of his family home in order to come and go at any hour. During the Christmas holidays, he announced his desire to divorce. He wanted to divest himself of any "distractions" so that he could totally focus on his heart's desire—politics.

Our culture adores those who demonstrate such devotion to their life ambition. We worship the athlete willing to pay whatever price necessary to win the competition. We promote the executive who neglects his personal life and health to work ninety hours a week. And we elect the politician who pays whatever price necessary to achieve greatness.

But God sees things differently. He labels as an idol anything that commands our complete attention and devotion. And He *hates* idols. Just listen to what God says about idolatry:

> You shall have no other gods before Me...for I, the LORD your God, am a jealous God. (Exodus 20:3, 5)

> And you shall love the LORD your God with all your heart and with all your soul and with all your might. (Deuteronomy 6:5)

> The LORD has issued a command concerning you: "Your name will no longer be perpetuated. I will cut off idol and image from the

house of your gods. I will prepare your grave, for you are con-
temptible." (Nahum 1:14)

For this you know with certainty, that no immoral or impure person
or covetous man, who is an idolater, has an inheritance in the
kingdom of Christ and God. (Ephesians 5:5)

God considers an idol as any thing or person we love more than Him.
Thus a goal or a dream that consumes our energy and thoughts can easily
become another god in our lives. When our ambition diverts our attention
from God in such a way, it's wrong.

Ambition is also wrong when...

2. It comes at the expense of others

Mark, the author of the second gospel, relates the story of two disciples who
wanted to climb to the top of their "profession" on the backs of their fellow
apostles. James and John, who were brothers, had obviously taken some
classes in self-assertiveness. They didn't hesitate to let Jesus know what they
wanted. "Grant that we may sit in Your glory, one on Your right, and one on
Your left" (Mark 10:37). When the other ten disciples heard what James and
John had requested, they became angry. So Jesus called the group together to
explain what a person must do to get ahead in God's eyes:

You know that those who are recognized as rulers of the Gentiles
lord it over them; and their great men exercise authority over them.
But it is not so among you, but whoever wishes to become great
among you shall be your servant; and whoever wishes to be first
among you shall be slave of all. For even the Son of Man did not
come to be served, but to serve, and to give His life a ransom for
many. (Mark 10:42–45)

James and John, like so many of us, thought they could only achieve their life goals by crushing the competition. But Jesus says no to that. He says that if we want to be truly great, we must become servants. The Greek word translated *servant* refers to a house servant whose chief responsibility is to render useful service to others in the home. The word *slave* refers to one who has forfeited his or her personal rights. Jesus says that the truly successful person focuses on meeting others' needs instead of clinging to his or her own personal rights. The person who puts others first will usually come out ahead in this world, and will always come out ahead in God's kingdom.

We see this truth demonstrated in the business world. How do you build a successful company? Not by becoming obsessed with driving your competition out of business, but by focusing your attention on providing the best product at the best possible price. Southwest Airlines is a good example of this principle. When Southwest began providing travel service in 1971, the company had only three airplanes serving three cities. But the company had a mission: provide air travel at a reasonable cost so people could afford to fly.

At that time, my dad worked for a rival airline determined to stamp Southwest out of business. First, my dad's airline tried to break Southwest financially by filing a mountain of lawsuits to keep the airline from flying. When that failed, my dad's company tried undercutting Southwest's fares, even though it meant losing millions of dollars. That didn't work either. Today, Southwest Airlines is one of the largest airlines in the country. And my dad's company? Bankrupt. His company went out of business over a decade ago and is now just a footnote in aviation history. As Southwest Airlines has proven, if you provide a valuable service to your customer, you won't have to worry about the competition.

We also see the superiority of servanthood in the government realm. Most people consider Abraham Lincoln our greatest president. If you read detailed accounts of his life, you'll discover that he was a very driven man. Lincoln had ambitious goals for his personal life and his presidency.

But Lincoln would willingly subjugate his personal agenda and rights for a greater purpose. Biographers tell of one occasion on which Lincoln visited General George McClellan, his general-in-chief. McClellan had been paralyzed with inactivity, and Lincoln wanted to persuade the general to start acting offensively. Not wanting to appear harsh, Lincoln thought a "kindlier and gentler" approach would be to visit the general in his own home. So, on the night of November 13, 1861, Lincoln and William Seward, the Secretary of State, went to McClellan's house. When they arrived, a servant informed President Lincoln and Secretary Seward that the general was at a wedding and would return shortly, and he ushered the visitors into the parlor to wait. About an hour later, McClellan returned home. After learning that the president was in the parlor waiting for him, the general marched upstairs and went to bed! The Secretary of State expressed outrage and demanded that Lincoln fire the general for such insubordination. But Lincoln kept his cool. "This is no time to be making points of etiquette and personal dignity. I would hold the reins of McClellan's horse if it would bring us victory."[5]

Lincoln was ambitious, but he'd subordinate his pride to achieve a greater purpose. He understood that true success came from serving others, not destroying them, and by his attitude, he avoided falling into sinful ambition.

Finally, ambition is wrong when...

3. It fails to allow for God's sovereignty

While the Bible never belittles planning, goal setting, and ambition, it does remind us that sometimes God has a different plan for our lives than we do. James' words come to mind:

> Come now, you who say, "Today or tomorrow, we shall go to such and such a city, and spend a year there and engage in business and make a profit." Yet you do not know what your life will be like tomorrow. You are just a vapor that appears for a little while and then vanishes away. Instead, you ought to say, "If the Lord wills, we shall live and also do this or that." But as it is, you boast in your arrogance; all such boasting is evil. (James 4:13–16)

James 4:13–16 doesn't condemn planning. Nothing is wrong with deciding to move one's business to another city to maximize profits. But, James says, we shouldn't formulate our plans without any regard for God's desires. When he suggests that we preface our plans with "If the Lord wills…," he doesn't mean for us to utter a stock phrase while we roll our eyes and proceed full-speed ahead with our own goals. Instead, James advises, we should realize that God may have completely different plans for us than we do. So before we immerse ourselves in our five-year business plans, we should understand that we might not even survive the night. (Remember the rich fool from chapter 3?) Our lives are extremely fragile, like a vapor or mist that appears and then suddenly vanishes. But most importantly, our omnipotent God holds our fragile lives in the palm of His hand, and we should allow Him to guide our ambitions.

To close this chapter, I'd like you to complete this sentence: "My greatest desire in life is to _____." Your answer may involve a position you'd like to achieve, a degree you'd like to earn, or a certain lifestyle you'd like to enjoy. Your greatest ambition might center around your dreams for a child or grandchild.

Having written your response, how can you tell whether your particular ambition has led (or might lead) you from God? To determine this, ask yourself these questions:

- Do I spend most of my free time thinking about this desire?
- Have I mistreated or neglected others (such as family members) in pursuit of this goal?
- How would I feel toward God if He said no to my desire?

Your honest answers to the above questions may reveal that you've unwittingly allowed your ambition to become a god in your life. If so, don't despair; this can easily happen to any of us. Nevertheless, we do need to remedy the situation and learn to keep our ambition in check. And the next chapter will talk about how.

....

CHAPTER 8

If It's Going to Be, It's Up to...Him

Keeping your goals from becoming your gods

I 'm going to decide to succeed."

"I'm not free till I believe in me."

"Make your thinking big enough for God to be in."

"If it's going to be, it's up to me."

The above statements come from a book on success I'm currently reading by America's premier "possibility thinker." I have to admit that such statements get my juices flowing quicker than my third cup of coffee every morning. I find something invigorating about dreaming and goal setting. Nothing wrong with that. The Bible advises us to wisely use the time God has given us. And the only way to use our time productively is to clearly define goals and pursue them.

As we saw in the last chapter, God gives us ambition. But like any healthy desire, ambition can become a lethal weapon that wars against our relationship with God when it leads to idolatry, competition, and pride. Yet, the desire to achieve can also powerfully motivate us to pursue true significance in life.

How can we productively channel our ambition? Let me list a few suggestions.

Develop a life-purpose bigger than yourself

Bobb Biehl has a great saying: "Every life exists for one of two purposes: to fill a greed or to meet a need." How true! Every person spends his or her life either focused on self or focused on others. In three of my previous books *(Choose Your Attitudes, Change Your Life,* and *The Road Most Traveled)*, I explain how and why we should develop a life-purpose statement. Without repeating much of that information, let me explain that a life-purpose statement simply answers the question, "Why do I exist?" If some people honestly answered that question, they'd say, "To make a lot of money," or "To have other people respect me," or "To enjoy life." All of those answers are examples of life-purposes built on "filling a greed." Yet no amount of money, respect, or pleasure can sufficiently fill the void of an empty life.

We need life-purposes bigger than ourselves that focus on "meeting a need." What needs do you see in the world or in others that spark your passion? What unique gifts do you possess to fulfill those needs? I believe God gives every person both a passion and a power to meet some specific need in the world; when you discover yours, you'll understand your life-purpose.

I love the words of George Bernard Shaw about the importance of having a life-purpose:

> This is the true joy in life…being used for a purpose recognized by yourself as a mighty one…being a force of Nature instead of a feverish selfish little clod of ailments and grievances complaining that the world will not devote itself to making you happy…I am of the opinion that my life belongs to the whole community and as long as I live it is my privilege to do for it whatever I can. I want to be thoroughly used up when I die. For the harder I work the more I live. I rejoice in life for its own sake. Life is no brief candle to me. It's a sort of splendid torch which I've got to hold up for the moment and I want to make it burn as brightly as possible before handing it on to future generations.[1]

Fortunately, a Christian already has a bigger purpose in life than peace, pleasure, and prosperity. The Westminster Shorter Catechism states it this way, "What is the chief end of man? Man's chief end is to glorify God and enjoy Him forever." Our life-purpose is to glorify God. What does that mean? It means to make God look bigger, better, and brighter to an unbelieving world. We must dedicate our lives to helping other people discover the joy of knowing God. When we make this our goal, we'll know we're using our ambition as God designed it.

Maintain balance in your life

In chapter 6, I suggested setting one goal for each of seven major life-areas: spiritual health, physical health, vocation, family, finances, social life, and personal growth. Such an exercise (and the resulting follow-through) will help guard against extremism in any one area. For example, you might form a family goal of spending fifteen minutes a night reading Bible stories to your children. That goal not only helps you instill spiritual values in your children, but it also safeguards against workaholism: To fulfill your goal, you must set aside work by your children's bedtime.

Or, you might have a financial goal of giving 10 percent of your income to the Lord's work each year. Giving that amount of money might prevent you from building your dream home in five years, but perhaps that isn't so bad. Building such a home might consume your thoughts and time, obscuring your focus on God. Your financial goal prevents that from happening.

Establishing goals for each life-area can keep you from becoming obsessed by any one ambition. If the politician we discussed in the last chapter had maintained balance in his life, he might not have risen to the top of his field. But neither would he have sacrificed his marriage and other important areas of his life.

Entrust your plans to God's sovereignty

Coming home to God doesn't require giving up your life's desires. Reestablishing an intimate relationship with Him doesn't mean you have to wander through life aimlessly waiting for a divine revelation about your next step. "Wait just a minute," I can hear some of you protesting. "We always suspected you were a heretic. Now we know for sure. Didn't Jesus say, 'For whoever wishes to save his life shall lose it; but whoever loses his life for My sake shall find it'?"

Yes, but as you examine Jesus' life you find that He had a very definite plan and purpose for His life. Many times people asked Jesus to do something, and He responded, "My hour has not come," a polite way of saying, "Sorry guys, but that isn't on the agenda." Jesus knew where He was headed in life. He had a plan. The key is that Jesus derived His agenda from His Heavenly Father. Jesus said, "My food is to do the will of Him who sent Me, and to accomplish His work" (John 4:34).

God also has a unique purpose for your life. How will He communicate that purpose to you? Through the Holy Spirit's leading. Paul wrote, "For all who are being led by the Spirit of God, these are the sons of God" (Romans 8:14). Sometimes the Holy Spirit leads us through insights we discover in the Bible. Sometimes He leads us through the wise counsel of others. And sometimes He leads us through our desires. When we truly seek to glorify God and we live obediently, we can expect God's desires to become our desires. The psalmist said, "Delight yourself in the Lord, and He will give you the desires of your heart" (Psalm 37:4). I used to think that verse meant that if I was spiritual enough, I could get God to do what I wanted Him to do. But I've discovered that the verse really means that when I live in harmony with my Heavenly Father, His ambitions become my ambitions; His goals become my goals; His desires become my desires.

Unfortunately, none of us can know for sure if our desires are *really* God's desires. So we must always entrust our plans to God's sovereignty. The Bible commands us to recognize that our plans are ultimately in God's hands:

The plans of the heart belong to man, but the answer of the tongue is from the LORD. (Proverbs 16:1)

Commit your works to the LORD, and your plans will be established. (Proverbs 16:3)

The mind of man plans his way, but the LORD directs his steps. (Proverbs 16:9)

Do you feel comfortable entrusting your future to God? Do you *really* believe His plan for your life is best?

The prodigal son's problem was that he really didn't trust his father. Like many children, he believed that his father wanted to make him miserable and prevent him from ever tasting success. Perhaps he imagined that his father was jealous of a son who might achieve more in his lifetime than the father ever would. Such doubts about his father's goodness caused the son to bolt from home. *If only I can get out from under his thumb, I can make something of myself,* he thought.

Like most children, the son failed to understand that nothing gives parents more pleasure than seeing their children succeed. Good parents don't feel threatened by their children's success; they long for it. The father had a plan for his son's future: The boy would gradually assume increasing responsibility in the family business, he and his brother would learn to work together, and one day the father would divide the estate in an orderly fashion. But the son didn't understand the plan nor did he trust the one who had designed it. So he left.

Perhaps you, too, have moved from your Father because you really don't understand His plan. You have specific goals and dreams for your life and yet, somewhere along the way, you embraced the myth that goals and godliness cannot coexist. Somebody told you that you must choose between ambition and obedience. Ambition won out, and you've lived in the far country ever since.

What a deceitfully clever ploy by the Enemy! He encourages you to make an unnecessary choice. God never asks you to abandon your ambitions. Philippians 2:13 says that God has endowed you with unique desires and special gifts to achieve more than you could possibly imagine. He has designed a plan both for your good and for His glory. He doesn't ask you to sacrifice your dreams but to submit them to His timetable and to His methods. And when you do, you'll be amazed how closely your deepest desires and God's eternal plan resemble one another. "For I know the plans that I have for you," declares the LORD, "plans for welfare and not for calamity to give you a future and a hope" (Jeremiah 29:11).

We've seen how money, pleasure, and ambition can easily lure us from God and into the far country. But why do so many Christians spend such a long time there? Why do we feel comfortable allowing our relationship with God to deteriorate for months, years, and even decades? A major reason is that we rarely hear the truth about sin.

PART TWO

Life in the Far Country

....

CHAPTER 9

The Truth about Sin

What three people teach us about life in the far country

Sin gets a lot of bad press, especially from us preacher types. We are always so negative, expounding on the downside of sin without giving equal time to some of its real benefits.

Benefits? Yes, you read it correctly. Life in the far country has its advantages, and I think we need to consider them. Why? Because I'm convinced that one reason we remain in the far country for so long is that we find it a much more pleasurable destination than we ever expected we would. While life in the far country isn't all pleasure, neither is it all pain.

Before we proceed to exposing the truth about sin, let's review what we've learned so far:

1. All Christians, at some point in their lives, will wander away from God. For some, the defection is sudden. For others, it occurs over a long period of time as a gradual erosion of their commitment. Some wander far away, others meander just a stone's throw from God-given boundaries, but we *all* drift. We can attribute our willingness to wander in part to our sin nature; we can attribute the rest to our Enemy who has developed a blueprint to destroy our relationship with God.

2. While Satan has custom-made a blueprint for the destruction of your spiritual life, he'll most likely use three of his most effective weapons: materialism, pleasure, and ambition. History has proven these tools amazingly effective in luring a believer away from the Heavenly Father.

We need to move this discussion from the abstract to the concrete, from the theoretical to the practical, by placing our relationship with God under the microscope of self-discovery. I'm not one given to contemplating my navel (at least for any extended period of time), but we have much to gain from occasionally asking ourselves some hard questions. A. W. Tozer has written, "Self-knowledge is so critically important to us in our pursuit of God and His righteousness that we live under a heavy obligation to do immediately whatever is necessary to remove the disguise and permit our real selves to be known."[1]

Using Tozer's perspective on self-discovery, let's diagnose the true condition of our spiritual lives. Take a few moments to answer the questions below. Be honest. You'll only gain the true benefit of this exercise by giving *honest* responses, not the answers you think others *expect.*

1. What do you want most in life?

2. What do you think about most often?

3. As you analyze your checkbook entries from the last month, what three items accounted for your greatest expenditures?

4. Think about your schedule for the past three days. Outside of work (in or outside of the home), what two activities consumed most of your time?

5. If you could spend one day being anyone else in the world, who would you be and why?

6. In the last week, how much time have you devoted to prayer and the study of God's Word?

7. As you look back over your spiritual life, when have you felt closest to God? When have you felt farthest away from Him? Where are you right now?

Taking the time to honestly answer these questions may be the most beneficial part of reading this book. If you've whizzed right by them, may I encourage you to go back and actually write down your responses. There are no right or wrong answers to these questions, but your responses can reveal the central focus of your life.

Perhaps your answer to the last question mirrored my own response a few years ago—you feel like you are in the "twilight zone" of your spiritual life. Maybe you can point to a time in your life when you were much closer to God than you are now, and you can also identify a time when you were farther away from Him. When I thought about question 7 a few years ago, I realized that I had been living in the far country for so long that I didn't even recognize it as a distant location. I had the gnawing sensation that something wasn't quite right, but I didn't know what to do about it.

I've noticed that most books and sermons deal with the process of moving away from God and/or the process of returning to God. But rarely does anyone address that "twilight zone" where the majority of Christians spend their time. As I said at the beginning of the chapter, one reason Christians live in that distant land for so long is that no one has ever told them the truth about it. The world tells us that life apart from God is filled with unending pleasure. Many preachers tell us that life apart from God is filled with unending pain. *Neither is completely true.*

I am writing this book not as an armchair theologian speculating about life apart from God but as someone like you who can point to a period—a long period—when I lived in the far country. Here are the lessons I learned through my experience:

1. It's not all pain;
2. It's not all pleasure; and
3. It can last a long time.

Three characters in the Old Testament illustrate these truths. All three share several characteristics. First, they were all committed believers who genuinely loved God. Second, they all allowed materialism, pleasure, and/or ambition to lure them away from God. Third, they all experienced major crises that could have destroyed their lives. And finally, they all enjoyed their own "homecoming." Let's look at these men individually and the truths we can learn from them.

SOLOMON: IT'S NOT ALL PAIN

Sometime ago I visited with a man who was living in the far country. He had become a Christian in his twenties, and his conversion had made an overnight difference in his life. He possessed an insatiable desire for studying God's Word, he attended church at every opportunity, and he gave generously to God's work in spite of his failing business.

Then came prosperity. Out of nowhere a major corporation offered a fortune for his small company. The man parlayed the substantial proceeds into considerable wealth through a combination of shrewd investment advice and just plain good fortune. Within a few years he became a multimillionaire. But as his riches increased, his spiritual hunger decreased. He dropped out of church, became involved in an illicit affair, and began to seriously question some of his foundational beliefs.

Trying to be a good pastor, I arranged to meet this man for lunch one day. I wanted to lure him back into the fold. But I made one basic mistake: describing what I thought his feelings *should* have been rather than what they actually were.

"Jack," I began, "we both know you are a long way from where you used to be spiritually. And although you are enjoying great success with your business, have beautiful homes around the country, and can buy anything you want, you know that something is missing in your life. I imagine that deep down you feel empty."

I will never forget the puzzled look on his face as he replied, "No, not really. I'm as happy as I have ever been."

Dumbfounded, I stumbled through a short prayer, looked at my watch, and "remembered" another appointment. Why don't these conversations ever turn out the way they're supposed to?

The truth is that my friend's experience is more the norm than most of us would like to admit. Living apart from God is a mixture of both pleasure and pain. And the pleasure, at least at the beginning, drowns out the pain.

No one illustrates that truth more than Solomon. He was the final king over the United Kingdom of Israel. He had watched his father David's kingdom end in tragedy because of David's gradual departure from God. I believe that Solomon intended to avoid making the same mistake in his own life. At the beginning of his reign, God appeared to Solomon at Gibeon and promised him anything he desired. Realizing his own inadequacy to rule over Israel, Solomon asked for divine wisdom: "And now, O LORD my God, Thou hast made Thy servant king in place of my father David, yet I am but a little child.... So give Thy servant an understanding heart to judge Thy people to discern between good and evil. For who is able to judge this great people of Thine?" (1 Kings 3:7, 9).

We can so quickly read those familiar verses without appreciating Solomon's extraordinary response. How many twenty-year-olds do you know who, given an opportunity to ask for anything, would have selected wisdom? Most young men would have asked for an unlimited credit line, a closet full of designer tunics, or the latest model chariot. But not Solomon. His heart was completely devoted to God. And God was so pleased with Solomon's choice that He not only granted him unparalleled wisdom, but He also threw in riches and power. There was only one catch. Solomon's future success would depend upon his continued devotion to God: "And if you walk in My ways, keeping My statues and commandments, as your father David walked, then I will prolong your days" (1 Kings 3:14).

For the next twenty years, Solomon kept his end of the bargain. God rewarded Solomon's complete obedience with great success in everything he did, climaxed by the building of the temple.

Immediately after the temple's completion, God appeared to Solomon again, and I don't think God's timing was haphazard. In my own life I've noticed that I'm most prone to wander from God after either a great failure or a great success. Failure causes us to question God's love. Success, however, causes us to question *our need* for God. That's why God waited until all the applause died down to remind Solomon...

> And as for you, if you will walk before Me as your father David
> walked, in integrity of heart and uprightness, doing according to all

that I have commanded you and will keep My statutes and My ordi-
nances, then I will establish the throne of your kingdom over Israel
forever, just as I promised to your father David…. But if you or your
sons shall indeed turn away from following Me, and shall not keep
My commandments…then I will cut Israel off from the land.
(1 Kings 9:4–7)

But Solomon failed to adhere to God's command. Like the prodigal son,
Solomon allowed ambition, materialism, and pleasure to destroy his relationship with his Father. First, in direct violation of God's command,
Solomon built a great army (1 Kings 10:26). Such an army gave Solomon
independence to do as he pleased, negating his dependence on God.

Second, he began to stockpile wealth, again directly violating God's laws.
First Kings 10:14 says that in one year Solomon accumulated 666 talents of
gold—worth about $320 million in today's currency. Like his power,
Solomon's wealth caused him to believe he was exempt from God's moral
codes.

And so, finally, in total disobedience to God's laws Solomon accumulated numerous wives and concubines. There were two problems with
Solomon's wives. First, he had too many of them! I believe God intentionally
prohibited kings from polygamy because it shifted their focus from the
spiritual to the sensual. Face it. You cannot prepare for a different sexual experience every night and simultaneously concentrate on the "affairs" of state.

Second, Solomon's wives were unbelievers who introduced him to the
worship of other gods. Scripture records that "when Solomon was old, his
wives turned his heart away after other gods; and his heart was not wholly
devoted to the LORD his God, as the heart of David his father had been"
(1 Kings 11:4).

Although 1 Kings compresses Solomon's downfall into one brief verse, it
actually occurred over a period of twenty years. We find a more detailed
account of those twenty years in Solomon's personal journal known as the
Book of Ecclesiastes:

I thought in my heart, "Come now, I will test you with pleasure to find out what is good." But that also proved to be meaningless. "Laughter," I said, "is foolish. And what does pleasure accomplish?" I tried cheering myself with wine, and embracing folly—my mind still guiding me with wisdom. I wanted to see what was worthwhile for men to do under heaven during the few days of their lives. I undertook great projects: I built houses for myself and planted vineyards. I made gardens and parks and planted all kinds of fruit trees in them. I made reservoirs to water groves of flourishing trees. I bought male and female slaves and had other slaves who were born in my house. I also owned more herds and flocks than anyone in Jerusalem before me. I amassed silver and gold for myself, and the treasure of kings and provinces. I acquired men and women singers, and a harem as well—the delights of the heart of man. I denied myself nothing my eyes desired; I refused my heart no pleasure.... Yet when I surveyed all that my hands had done and what I had toiled to achieve, everything was meaningless, a chasing after the wind; nothing was gained under the sun (Ecclesiastes 2:1–8, 10–11, NIV).

You might ask, "Isn't Solomon saying that his years living apart from God were filled with misery and emptiness?" Not at the time. Remember, Solomon wrote these words in his later years. As he looked back on his life, he had the proper perspective: Life apart from God was empty. But it took him *years* to reach that conclusion. Solomon wouldn't have spent so long in the far country had it been a totally miserable existence.

Stop and think about that for a moment. No one with any sense (and don't forget that Solomon was the wisest man in the world) would choose to endure a life of total unhappiness for twenty years. If you touch a hot stove, you don't keep your finger on it until you figure out some other course of action. You remove your finger as quickly as possible.

It's the same way with sin. If sin brought nothing but pain, none of us would indulge in it for very long. We are too self-centered to endure anything that only brings pain.

The Bible is completely honest about this. God's Word never paints sin as unpleasurable. In describing Moses' faith, the writer of Hebrews says, "By faith Moses, when he had grown up, refused to be called the son of Pharaoh's daughter; choosing rather to endure ill-treatment with the people of God, than to enjoy the passing *pleasures* of sin" (Hebrews 11:24–25, emphasis mine). The pleasure of sin may be temporary, but it is also real.

Let's return to the prodigal son for a moment. Why did he remain away from home for so long? If he had been robbed his first night away from home, had been ridiculed by the prostitutes with whom he first slept, and had vomited his first drink of alcohol, he probably would have returned home rather quickly. But life in the far country, at least at first, was more enjoyable than he had imagined.

DAVID: IT'S NOT ALL PLEASURE

Yesterday I counseled one of our church members who had deserted his wife and two small sons because he no longer felt fulfilled in his marriage. Although he had no biblical grounds for the divorce, he was convinced that God did not want him to be unhappy for the rest of his life. When, several months ago, he originally told me of his decision to leave his family, I assured him that I would pray for him, not just a general "God, bless Bill" prayer but a prayer like this: "God, I pray that You would completely bankrupt Bill, that he would lose his job, that his friends would desert him, and that You would fill his mind with so much anxiety and guilt that he won't be able to sleep at night." (You can probably understand why my counseling load isn't that heavy.)

When Bill came to see me yesterday, I asked him how he was doing. He replied, "I have started dating Michelle, and in one sense I have never been happier. And yet, I have never been more miserable. Apparently God has been answering your prayers." He then shared how the contentious divorce and child-support payments had nearly bankrupted him, how his friends from church wouldn't associate with him, and how his children despised him. "I wake up in the middle of the night sometimes thinking I am having a heart attack." God does answer prayer!

Bill's experience is not unique. When we look at King David's life we discover that he, too, spent a long period of time in the far country. We've already detailed his experience with Bathsheba on that hot summer night in Jerusalem. In a later chapter we'll explore how God used a crisis to bring David back home. But what about the time after David's departure and before his return? Let's look at how David described that period of time:

When I kept silent about my sin, my body wasted away
Through my groaning all day long.
For day and night Thy hand was heavy upon me;
My vitality was drained away as with the fever heat of summer.

(Psalm 32:3–4)

Make no mistake about it: David felt exhilarated by his continuing sexual relationship with Bathsheba—he even took her as his own wife. This was no "one-night stand"! But at the same time, David had this gnawing sensation that he would have to pay for his actions. The God David had known since his childhood was not about to let him get away with this. Judgment would come. The question was not if, but when.

Perhaps the most painful aspect about life in the far country is the anxiety it induces. Regardless of the reasons or extent of our departure, we know that God won't allow us to stay away. We feel as though the sword of Damocles hangs over our heads, ready to drop at any moment. We begin to interpret illness, financial reversals, friction in relationships, or problems at work as God's judgment against us.

My nine-year-old daughter, Julia, enjoys the thrill of roller coasters, scary movies, and rousing games of hide-and-seek. The other night I thought I'd feed her capacity for thrill by hiding in her bedroom closet. When she came into the room, I jumped out and yelled, "Boo." She screamed and then began to laugh uncontrollably. But when bedtime came, she didn't want to go to sleep by herself. She kept thinking I would jump out of the closet at any moment. So she insisted on keeping the lights on and checking my location every five minutes, even though I had promised not to scare her again. She had a difficult time going to sleep for the next week, not because of what I was actually doing, but because of her fear of what I *might* do.

I believe David experienced that same kind of fear every night after Bathsheba drifted off to sleep and he began to obsess about what God *might* do to him. Would God strike him with some painful illness? Would He publicly humiliate him? Would Bathsheba leave him for another man? Would he lose the position he had spent a lifetime pursuing? These questions weighed heavily on David and drained his physical strength. Whatever pleasure he derived from Bathsheba was severely diluted by the nagging fear of impending judgment.

Moses: It Can Last a Long Time

We don't know for sure how long the prodigal son spent in the distant country. He may have stayed six months, a year, or even longer. But please note that the major catalyst for the son's return was his lack of financial resources. Had Daddy's money lasted, the son would have remained in the far country much longer. It took a crisis to precipitate his return.

The fact that we can spend months and even years living in the far country, without any severe consequences, can be very confusing. Solomon, who spent at least twenty years of his life away from God, expressed that perplexity well when he wrote, "Because the sentence against an evil deed is not executed quickly, therefore the hearts of the sons of men among them are given fully to do evil" (Ecclesiastes 8:11). Allow me to paraphrase Solomon's thought: "Because God doesn't zap us immediately when we step out of line, we wander farther and farther away." When we do not feel the immediate sting of God's judgment in our lives, we think that maybe God doesn't really care about sin or maybe He doesn't even exist.

Perhaps you've had similar thoughts recently. You know you are far away from God, whether a few steps out of His will or as far away as you've ever been. Your life in the far country may include blatant immorality such as David's or, more likely, it is characterized by an everyday disregard for God.

Does God not care? Is He too impotent to really do anything? Is He even there? I think there are at least two reasons that God doesn't always discipline us immediately for our disobedience:

The patience of God

This Sunday night we're playing "Stump the Pastor" at our church. Over the last few weeks people have submitted questions they'd like me to answer. Some of these questions are amusing ("What do you wear underneath your waders when you baptize?"), some are unanswerable ("Please *briefly* explain the doctrine of predestination."), and some are predictable ("Why does God allow evil to go unpunished in the world?").

That last question is easy to answer because 2 Peter 3:9 clearly addresses it. In this verse Peter explains the Lord's delay in returning to earth to punish the wicked: "The Lord is not slow about His promise, as some count slowness, but is patient toward you, not wishing for any to perish but for all to come to repentance."

Although this verse refers specifically to the punishment of unbelievers, the principle also applies to believers living apart from God. The Lord is patient. The word translated *patient* literally means long-tempered. To understand the concept of being long-tempered, picture the opposite of short-tempered. We all know people who have a short fuse. The slightest irritation—a red light, a forgotten birthday, a slow driver ahead—sets off a nuclear explosion.

But God isn't like that. He willingly endures mistreatment and estrangement by His creatures in the hope that they will return.

The purpose of God

Moses spent a significant amount of time in the far country. Although God had promised to make Moses the great liberator of Israel, by the time he reached his fortieth birthday, he began to think that dream would go unfulfilled. According to Acts 7:23–25, Moses decided to start the revolt against Egypt himself by killing an Egyptian soldier. Big mistake. The Bible records that Moses spent the next forty years of his life fleeing the wrath of Pharaoh by living as "an alien in the land of Midian" (Acts 7:29).

The Bible is virtually silent about those forty years Moses spent on the backside of the desert—except for one verse. In describing that desert experience, Moses later wrote, "He found him in a desert land, and in the howling waste of a wilderness; He encircled him, He cared for him, He guarded him as the pupil of His eye" (Deuteronomy 32:10).

Although Moses' life in the far country resulted from his own disobedience, God used that experience to teach Moses some invaluable lessons about faith, obedience, and God's provision. Moses probably thought God was through with him forever, but in fact God used that time to prepare Moses for an even greater work. After Moses' forty years in the distant land, God allowed him to return home and experience the greatest years of his life.

You may have lived in that distant country for a long time. Like Moses, you have no one to blame but yourself. You've allowed a thirst for success, an illicit affair, a destructive habit, or maybe just the ordinary concerns of everyday life to take you away from your Heavenly Father. I know how it is. I spent about seven years in that desert myself. And though I regret the length of time I spent there, in a strange way, I'm also grateful for it. For during my time in the far country I learned some lessons about faith, obedience, and forgiveness that I could have never learned anywhere else.

And so can you.

Life in the far country isn't all pain, isn't all pleasure, and can last a long time. God can even use your time away from Him to teach you important truths about Himself. But He won't allow you to remain there for long without experiencing some major disruptions. In the next chapter we will discover how God speaks to those of us in the far country.

C H A P T E R   1 0

....

Intervention

Why God refuses to play fair

W e surveyed one hundred ministers and asked them, 'Is it all right to tell a child that if he is bad, God will punish him?' How many ministers said yes?"

I faced this question as a participant in a nationally televised game show. My opponent jumped to answer it, relegating to the Dark Ages the idea of God punishing people. She argued that the answer had to be a low number.

Then it was my turn.

"Robert, you're a preacher," the host reminded me and the millions watching. "What do you think?"

I hesitated.

During those microseconds, my mind raced back to what my parents used to tell me to keep me in line: "If you ever _____ (one of any number of sins), lightning will strike you dead." I also thought about the number of passages in both the Old and New Testaments that spoke clearly about the issue. Yet, I had to admit there was something distasteful about the idea of an omnipotent God picking on finite and helpless people, especially children. The last thing the American viewing public needed was another negative image of a preacher. So I hedged my answer.

Had the writer of Hebrews been in my place on one of America's most popular game shows, however, he wouldn't have hesitated at all. In Hebrews 12, the author speaks clearly about how God works in the lives of those who have allowed materialism, pleasure, and/or ambition to captivate their affections:

My son, do not regard lightly the discipline of the LORD, nor faint when you are reproved by Him; for those whom the LORD loves He disciplines, and He scourges every son whom He receives. It is for discipline that you endure; God deals with you as with sons; for what son is there whom his father does not discipline? But if you are without discipline, of which all have become partakers, then you are illegitimate children and not sons…. All discipline for the moment seems not to be joyful, but sorrowful; yet to those who have been trained by it, afterwards it yields the peaceful fruit of righteousness (Hebrews 12:5–8, 11).

Up to this point we've considered:

1. Why we wander away from God (Satan's plan coupled with our bent toward sin);
2. How we wander away from God (by pursuing materialism, pleasure, and ambition); and
3. What life is like away from God (a curious blend of pleasure and pain that we might indulge in for a long time).

As we've considered these three areas, the story of the prodigal son has served as a useful illustration of a Christian's departure from and return to God. But the analogy breaks down in one place: the father's response. As we read the story, we find the father waiting patiently for the return of his son. "But while he was still a long way off, his father saw him, and felt compassion for him, and ran and embraced him, and kissed him" (Luke 15:20).

We find appealing this image of a waiting father, and it serves Jesus' purpose of portraying God's immense love. However, though God is patient, He is not passive. God doesn't sit in heaven twiddling His thumbs wondering when we might realize the emptiness of our pursuits, the error of our ways, and return home.

Instead, God actively pursues us. And He doesn't always play fair. If you're living in the far country, beware. Without apology, God will marshal His considerable power against you. He will manipulate other people and circumstances to bring excruciating pain into your life. His motive? To bring you home.

REPROOFS FOR OUR RETURN

We're going to explore how God uses difficult circumstances and people to bring us back to Him. The Bible has a term for this process: *reproof.* A reproof is simply a difficult circumstance God allows in our lives to teach us a lesson. We can either ignore God's reproofs or we can learn from them.

> He is on the path of life who heeds instruction, but he who forsakes reproof goes astray. (Proverbs 10:17)

> Whoever loves discipline loves knowledge, but he who hates reproof is stupid. (Proverbs 12:1)

> Poverty and shame will come to him who neglects discipline, but he who regards reproof will be honored. (Proverbs 13:18)

> Stern discipline is for him who forsakes the way; he who hates reproof will die. (Proverbs 15:10)

> A man who hardens his neck after much reproof will suddenly be broken beyond remedy. (Proverbs 29:1)

The captain of an airliner has all kinds of on-board computers and warning systems to help him fly the plane. If the aircraft experiences an engine fire, loses too much altitude, or veers too closely to another plane, alarms and even computer-generated voices alert him to the danger. Still, the pilot ultimately must decide whether or not to heed the warning. His decision not only impacts his life but also the lives of the passengers and crew members on board with him.

It's the same way with God's reproofs. As a pastor, I'm always amazed at people's ability to ignore the reproofs God sends into their lives to warn them that they're seriously off course. They regard bankruptcies, failed marriages, rebellious children, and illnesses as life's trials rather than God's reproofs.

Obviously, not all our hardships are the result of God's discipline. Some problems result from living in a fallen world. Other problems are the price we pay for living a God-honoring life. God sometimes allows trials in our lives to strengthen us or to help us minister to other Christians who may face similar problems. Often we struggle to discern God's purpose in allowing a particular difficulty in our lives. When we don't know His reasons, we need to ask for His wisdom. James wrote, "Consider it all joy, my brethren, when you encounter various trials; knowing that the testing of your faith produces endurance. And let endurance have its perfect result, that you may be perfect and complete, lacking in nothing. But if any of you lacks wisdom, let him ask of God, who gives to all men generously and without reproach, and it will be given to him" (James 1:2–5).

As we seek His wisdom, we may find that He *is* using a certain trial as a reproof in our lives. Let's consider several different reproofs God may bring to someone living in the far country.

Financial pressure

Living in the far country can be very expensive. If you don't believe it, just ask the prodigal son. After receiving his portion of his father's estate, he traveled to the far country and "squandered his estate with loose living. Now when he had spent everything, a severe famine occurred in that country, and he began to be in need" (Luke 15:13–14).

Some people wonder how anyone could so ignorantly spend their entire inheritance in the course of several weeks, months, or even years. Didn't this guy realize that his money would eventually run out? But if you carefully reread the text, you might find the prodigal son a pretty good planner. When he asked his father for his share of the estate, I think he knew exactly how much money that would be. Although he quickly spent his money on prostitutes and loose living, it didn't matter. He had a plan. When the money ran out, he'd find a job to support his lifestyle. And even if it took him awhile to find a job, his new friends would support him.

But one contingency arose that he didn't foresee: a famine. When a severe famine struck the land, his job opportunities dried up. His friends, consumed with their own needs, deserted him. He was left to fend for himself. The best he could do was to beg a stranger for a job feeding pigs. One can hardly imagine a job more humiliating for a nice Jewish boy. Only when he found himself fantasizing about eating pig slop did he realize the absurdity of his situation. Financial hardship motivated him to reexamine his life.

Charles Colson, one of the most revered Christian statesmen of our generation, used to have a plaque on his wall in his pre-Christian, Nixon White House days. The plaque read, "When you've got them by the [sensitive part of the male anatomy], their hearts and minds will follow." Regarding God's use of financial hardship in our lives, we could adapt that crude saying to "When God has got you by your pocketbook, your heart and mind will follow."

When we focus our hearts and minds on someone or something other than God, He often uses financial pressure to show us how unworthy that person or object is of our affection. Consider, for example, a man who spends several years of his life in an illicit affair. He pours all of his creative energy and discretionary income into romancing a woman other than his wife. Once the relationship is uncovered, his wife divorces him, and he faces attorney costs, child-support payments, alimony, and the maintenance of two residences. Perhaps Solomon had this kind of financial pressure in mind when he wrote, "For on account of a harlot one is reduced to a loaf of bread" (Proverbs 6:26). Wandering away from home can be expensive.

However, living in the far country doesn't always involve blatant sins such as adultery. As we've seen in previous chapters, Satan often uses idolatry to turn our hearts away from God. Again, God frequently uses financial pressure to remind us how expensive our idols are.

Consider the couple who wants nothing more than to build their dream home in the country. Both husband and wife know that the payments on such a home are out of their reach, but they justify the expense by promising to cut back in other areas and expecting healthy raises to ease the pressure. The building of that home consumes them for the next year. They excuse their lack of involvement in ministry and the cessation of their personal devotional times by saying, "Our lives are so frantic right now, but when things slow down…" But they never do.

Once in their home, this husband and wife discover that instead of decreasing, their expenses have increased dramatically. Unanticipated repairs, landscaping costs, increased utilities eat up their discretionary income. And the expected raises never materialize. Instead of owning a new home, their new home owns them—and it's not nearly as beautiful as it was in the blueprints.

Amazingly, this couple fails to draw the connection between their financial difficulties and their idolatry. They have not profited from the reproofs of life.

Family pressure

If God cannot get our attention through our wallets, He may speak to us through our families. He may use the alienation of our mates to reach us. In his book *Descending into Greatness,* Bill Hybels tells the story of a church member whose work had become his idol. As a bond trader on the Chicago Board of Trade, Lance Murdock found himself working fifteen-hour days during the early years of his marriage. Frustrated by his neglect, Murdock's wife had an affair. Hybels writes,

> He never got over [the affair]. He had lost her, his ultimate possession, to another man. Even if it was over, there still was the bitter taste in his mouth. They began to grow in different directions. Lance was still determined to enjoy his success, even if she did not want to. He traveled to Myrtle Beach for golf, Las Vegas for gambling, Florida for the sun. "I ran our marriage right into the ground."[1]

The pain of that divorce, coupled with severe financial losses, awakened Lance Murdock to his spiritual bankruptcy.

Other times God uses a child's rebellion as a powerful reproof. I think of a friend in a former church who had allowed his career to become the god of his life. During lunches together, he'd freely admit that he was drifting in his relationship with God. But he didn't fall to his knees until he discovered his eighteen-year-old son's involvement in drugs and repudiation of the Christian faith.

"How could my son rebel against me and against God?" he asked me. I didn't want to stick the knife in too deeply. My friend was already bleeding, but he needed to hear the truth. "Ron, for the last five years Jeff has seen you rebelling against your Heavenly Father. Where do you think he learned it?" Fortunately, Ron knew the answer before I pointed it out, and he made some positive corrections in his life.

Illness

Another way God speaks to those living in the far country is through sickness. As we discuss this truth, we need to be very careful. Some would say that *all* sickness is the result of personal sin. (Remember Job's "friends"?) But a simple study of God's Word disproves that notion. The Bible tells us that God allows sickness for at least three distinct reasons.

First, some sickness is given to lead to death. For a Christian, death is simply a transition from this life to the eternal state God has prepared for us. If our bodies never deteriorated, we'd be trapped in this world forever. For this reason, I often have a difficult time getting excited when someone shares a healing he or she has experienced. No matter how miraculous such a healing is, it's only temporary. God's ultimate plan is that we rid ourselves of these temporal bodies so that we might inherit the new bodies He has prepared for us. And He often uses the tool of illness to effect that transition.

Second, some sickness is given for God's glory. The apostle Paul was afflicted with a physical illness he referred to as his "thorn in the flesh." After God refused his request for healing on three different occasions, Paul concluded:

"Most gladly, therefore, I will rather boast about my weaknesses, that the power of Christ may dwell in me" (2 Corinthians 12:9). Paul understood that through our weakness, not our strength, God can most clearly demonstrate His power. My mother was a living example of how God can use illness for His glory. Between the time she was diagnosed with cancer and her death six months later, she demonstrated the supernatural peace available to a Christian facing death.

Third, some sickness is the result of personal sin. Numbers 12 records Miriam being struck with leprosy because of her disobedience. A similar illness befell Gehazi, the servant of Elisha, because of his greed. David admitted that his refusal to acknowledge his sin with Bathsheba resulted in some adverse physical effects: "When I kept silent about my sin, my body wasted away through my groaning all day long" (Psalm 32:3).

I believe that James had this kind of sin in view when he wrote: "Is anyone among you sick? Let him call for the elders of the church, and let them pray over him, anointing him with oil in the name of the Lord; and the prayer offered in faith will restore the one who is sick, and the Lord will raise him up, and if he has committed sins, they will be forgiven him. Therefore, confess your sins to one another, and pray for one another, so that you may be healed" (James 5:14–16).

James isn't saying that all sickness is the result of sin—but some of it is. Think about this for a moment. Has God changed in the last three thousand years?

"No," you'd say. "He is the same yesterday, today, and forever." I agree. So how did God deal with His own children, the Israelites, when they wandered away from Him? He used the bite of fiery serpents, leprosy, and even death to warn His people. Why should we think He would work any differently today? We just have different names for the plagues that afflict us: cancer, heart disease, AIDS…

When discerning the cause of someone else's illness, we need to be very careful. Jesus' disciples made a quick judgment about the cause of a blind man's infirmity, and their diagnosis was erroneous (John 9:1–4). However, when illness strikes us, we need to prayerfully consider whether that illness could be one of God's reproofs.

THREE PRINCIPLES ABOUT GOD'S DISCIPLINE

As we've just seen, God's correction in the life of a wandering believer comes in various forms. But three principles about His discipline apply to all of us.

God's correction is impartial

Imagine that you and I are standing on top of a tall building. You are an obedient Christian; I am a Christian living in the far country. In a moment of insanity, we both jump off the building. Which one of us is exempt from the law of gravity? Easy answer. *Splat! Splat!* Neither of us.

In the same way, none of us is immune from God's discipline. Some Christians don't realize this. They think they're exempt from experiencing God's reproofs because of:

- a dramatic conversion experience many years ago;
- their involvement in ministry; or
- godly parents or grandparents.

But often the opposite is true: Those who have walked closest to God frequently face His most severe discipline. Paul explains this truth in 1 Corinthians. Because of the growth, orthodoxy, and influence of their church, the Corinthians thought they were immune from God's discipline. But Paul quickly cleared their minds of that misconception by reminding them of the way God dealt with Israel:

> For I do not want you to be unaware, brethren, that our fathers were all under the cloud, and all passed through the sea; and all were baptized into Moses in the cloud and in the sea; and all ate the same spiritual food; and all drank the same spiritual drink, for they were drinking from a spiritual rock which followed them; and the rock was Christ. Nevertheless, with most of them God was not well

pleased; for they were laid low in the wilderness (1 Corinthians 10:1–5).

Perhaps you, too, have been deluded in your thinking. You know you've been living apart from God for some time, and you've convinced yourself that you're immune to the kind of financial difficulties, family problems, and illnesses that afflict other Christians because of some special *understanding* between you and God. Before you persist in that thinking, remember what happened to the Israelites.

No group of people had ever enjoyed such an intimate relationship with God. First, they had experienced *supernatural deliverance*. For four hundred years, God's people cried for deliverance from the Egyptian bondage. God heard their cry, and Exodus 14 records the miraculous event of God parting the Red Sea for the Israelites as Pharaoh's army pursued them. From that moment on, whenever the people started to doubt God, Israel's leaders would remind them of that landmark event of deliverance that proved they were God's chosen people.

Second, the Israelites received *supernatural revelation*. Paul says that they were "baptized into Moses," having had Moses as their leader. Moses received God's supernatural revelation on Mount Sinai and delivered it to the Israelites. Unlike the surrounding nations, the Israelites knew God's thinking on a variety of issues through His law.

Finally, the Israelites experienced God's *supernatural provision*. Can you remember times in your life when God miraculously provided for your needs? Maybe you received an unexpected, but severely needed, check in the mail; perhaps a new job suddenly opened up when every door seemed closed; or possibly you experienced reconciliation in a fractured relationship. Most of us have a few of those times that assure us that God holds us in His hands.

The Israelites had a few of these experiences too. Their supernatural provision came in the wilderness when they were hungry and thirsty. Exodus 16–17 tells us that, in the middle of the desert, God miraculously provided food and water for them.

Yet, in spite of their experiences of supernatural deliverance, revelation, and provision, the Bible says, "Nevertheless, with most of them God was not well pleased; for they were laid low in the wilderness" (1 Corinthians 10:5).

Although we briefly touched on this verse in chapter 5, let's examine it more closely. A paraphrase of this verse might read: "Although they were God's chosen people, He was not pleased with them and therefore covered the wilderness with their corpses." This 1 Corinthians verse refers to the story of Israel's rebellion described in Numbers 14. Because the Israelites lacked faith, God decided to eternally curse them. Moses prayed on their behalf, and God relented, deciding not to curse them. But He'd still allow them to suffer the consequences of their unbelief. "Surely all the men who have seen My glory and My signs, which I performed in Egypt and in the wilderness, yet have put Me to the test these ten times and have not listened to My voice, shall by no means see the land which I swore to their fathers, nor shall any of those who spurned Me see it. Your corpses shall fall in this wilderness..." (Numbers 14:22–23, 29).

A few years ago, the northeastern portion of our country was hit by a tremendous hurricane. Television newscasts featured footage of the hurricane's path of destruction. As a helicopter flew over the disaster site, you could see boats, houses, and cars strewn over the landscape. The pictures provided a sobering reminder of nature's—and, more importantly, God's—power.

As we discussed in chapter 5, if you could have flown over the wilderness area three thousand years ago, you'd have seen an equally sobering sight: thousands of Israelite corpses covering the landscape. How could God do such a thing to His own people, to those upon whom He'd previously bestowed great blessings?

We find the answer in God's impartiality. Although the Israelites had received supernatural salvation, revelation, and provision, they still fell away from God and, as a result, forfeited their physical lives. Their corpses were scattered in the wilderness as a monument to the consequences of disobedience.

We can look around today and see the "bodies" of fellow Christians who have likewise sinned and faced God's discipline. Almost everyone reading this book can think of pastors, church leaders, and laymen who have fallen into immorality, carnality, rebellion, and unbelief and have reaped the consequences. Like the Israelites, they mistakenly believed that because they had experienced God's blessings in the past, they were exempt from His discipline.

In 1 Corinthians 10:1–5, Paul reminds both the Corinthians and us of God's complete impartiality. God hasn't changed in three thousand years. He has no more tolerance for disobedience today than He did then.

God's discipline is restorative

The writer of Hebrews carefully chooses his words to explain God's correction. He writes, quoting from Proverbs 3:12, "For those whom the LORD loves He reproves…" Notice that he doesn't say *condemn* but *reproves*. What's the difference?

When a murderer is condemned to die, there's obviously no thought of restoration in his sentencing. He has committed a heinous crime that demands a severe sentence. The murderer suffers the consequences of his action.

Although murder is just about the only crime in our society punishable by the death sentence, God has a higher code of conduct. *Any* infraction of God's law results in eternal death or separation from God. Paul wrote, "For the wages of sin is death" (Romans 6:23). Adultery, idolatry, greed, and lying are all capital offenses demanding eternal death according to God's penal code.

But the gospel says that when we become Christians, God commutes our sentences. When we trust in Christ for our forgiveness, we receive complete pardon for our offenses. As Paul confidently asserts in Romans 8:1, "There is therefore now no condemnation for those who are in Christ Jesus." Why? Because we're no longer God's enemies; instead, we're His children!

But that change in status doesn't exempt us from God's discipline; in fact, our new status guarantees it! That's what the writer of Hebrews has in mind when he explains: "It is for discipline that you endure; God deals with you as with sons; for what son is there whom his father does not discipline?… He disciplines us for our good, that we may share His holiness" (Hebrews 12:7, 10). Let me offer another Jeffress paraphrase: "The fact that God doesn't allow you to get away with anything is proof that you are really His child!"

I never understood (or believed) my parents introductory "this-hurts-me-more-than-it-hurts-you" speech before they whacked me…until I became a parent myself. Those of you who are parents understand how difficult and painful it is to punish your children. Most of us battle being too lenient with our kids. We find it much easier to allow offenses to slide than to deal with them. Yet we realize that allowing wrong attitudes, sassy replies, and broken rules to go unpunished now could result in greater problems in the future. Our discipline indicates our concern for our children.

So does God's. The fact that He refuses to allow us to wander too far away without experiencing financial pressure, family disruption, illness, or some other correction is evidence that we really do belong to Him. "But if you are without discipline…then you are illegitimate children and not sons" (Hebrews 12:8).

God's discipline is instructional

Whatever reproof God sends into your life is primarily for your benefit. But God also disciplines you to warn *others* about the dangers of disobedience. For example, Acts 5 records the story of two Christians, Ananias and Sapphira, who lied to God and to the church about the money they planned to contribute to the offering. Because of their sin, God struck them dead in front of the entire church. Luke reports that afterwards "great fear came upon the whole church, and upon all who heard of these things" (Acts 5:11). What an understatement! I have often thought that Peter could have taken the largest offering in the history of the church had he passed the plate right then! (We pastors are prone to thinking that way.)

Similarly, Paul says that God punished the Israelites to teach future generations about the consequences of disobedience: "Now these things happened to them as an example, and they were written for our instruction..." (1 Corinthians 10:11).

"If you want to know how God deals with His children who are living in the far country, look at and learn from the Israelites," Paul says. Viewing calamity in others' lives should make us especially sensitive to warnings.

One night I was sitting in an airplane parked at a gate at the Dallas/Fort Worth airport, getting ready to depart for San Diego. As we prepared to taxi from the gate, I looked out the window at the jetliner parked at the adjacent gate. Suddenly, I noticed a bright orange flame shoot up from the plane's wing. "Did you see that?" I asked the man seated next to me.

"No," he responded curtly.

About thirty seconds later, I saw the same thing again. I stopped a flight attendant busily preparing for our departure and said, "Pardon me, but I think the airplane next to us is on fire!"

"That couldn't be," she tried to assure me.

No sooner had those words left her lips than the whole wing of that plane erupted in flames. The back door of the jet bolted open, the inflatable slide popped out, and the passengers came hurtling out of the plane.

After a considerable delay caused by the emergency equipment, our plane finally started taxiing down the runway. When the flight attendant began her customary, and usually ignored, instructions concerning emergency exits and procedures, she had an unusually attentive audience. Passengers who usually read or conversed during such warnings hung on every word. Some were even taking notes! Why? Because having just witnessed a disaster, they were particularly sensitive to warnings.

Have you experienced your own share of "disasters" recently? Are you wondering why you've been overwhelmed recently by financial pressure, family problems, illness, or some other difficulty? Don't label every problem in your life as bad luck. And don't gloat over others' misfortunes. Instead, realize that God often speaks to those of us in the far country through discipline, both in our lives and in the lives of others.

PART THREE

The Return

....

CHAPTER 11

The Journey Home

How crisis and repentance can turn our hearts back to God

I suspect that many of you reading this book have agreed with most everything you have read. You understand that you have an external Enemy and an internal drive that constantly pull you away from God. You reluctantly admit that those two forces have successfully dulled your relationship with Him. You agree that life in the far country is a curious blend of pain and pleasure. And as you survey the circumstances of your life over the past few years, you understand that God has tried to get your attention through financial, relational, or physical difficulties.

I once saw an advertisement for a book that said, "This book is for those who are sick and tired of being sick and tired." I believe you probably purchased this book because you're sick and tired of living your life apart from God. You're tired of that low-grade, but constant, feeling that all is not right between you and God. You're tired of fearing what disaster God might send your way to summon your attention; of worrying about what destiny awaits you on the other side of the grave; of relentlessly chasing after materialism, pleasure, and ambition.

You want to come home. You desire the intimacy and vitality that once characterized your spiritual life. The only question is, "How?"

How can God rekindle a heart that has grown cold?

How can I expect God to completely forgive me?

How can I ever make up for the lost time I've spent in the far country?

How can I be sure that if I do return to God, I will remain?

I believe similar thoughts crossed the prodigal son's mind as he labored in the pigpen:

Will my father accept me if I return?

If I return, will I be treated as a slave or a son?

What about the inheritance—have I lost it forever, or will my father give me more?

Am I a hypocrite for wanting to return home since I feel no special love for my father?

What if life in my father's house proves unbearable—where do I go then?

Let's return to our story for a moment and look at the steps that took the younger son from the pigpen back to his father's home:

> And he was longing to fill his stomach with the pods that the swine were eating, and no one was giving anything to him. But when he came to his senses, he said, "How many of my father's hired men have more than enough bread, but I am dying here with hunger! I will get up and go to my father, and will say to him, 'Father, I have sinned against heaven, and in your sight; I am no longer worthy to be called your son; make me as one of your hired men.'" And he got up and came to his father. (Luke 15:16–20)

This story, coupled with my own experience as a pastor and Christian, illustrates four factors necessary to experience a genuine homecoming:

Crisis;

Repentance;

Forgiveness; and

Perseverance.

Let's first take a closer look at the role crisis plays in encouraging us to return to our Father.

CRISIS

I've never known a Christian to return from the far country without first experiencing a tremendous crisis in his or her life. God uses problems to speak to us. C. S. Lewis once wrote, "Pain is God's megaphone. He whispers to us in our pleasure, but shouts to us in our pain."

The great Christian statesman Malcolm Muggeridge paid this tribute to the value of pain in a Christian's life: "Contrary to what might be expected, I look back on experiences that at the time seemed especially desolating and painful with particular satisfaction. Indeed, I can say with complete truthfulness that everything I have learned in my seventy-five years in this world, everything that has truly enhanced and enlightened my existence, has been through affliction from our earthly existence."

That one-in-a-million Christian who has never traveled to the far country and felt the heavy hand of God dealing blow after painful blow might find Muggeridge's words peculiar. How could anyone look back on painful times with "particular satisfaction"? I don't believe Muggeridge is claiming that we will ever label such experiences as enjoyable. But if those deep hurts result in our homecoming, one day we'll view them from a different perspective. Let me illustrate what I mean.

My wife, Amy, attended the University of Texas, and I was a student at Baylor University. One Saturday during our freshman year, Amy visited me in Waco to watch Baylor battle Texas for the Southwest Conference Football Championship. After the first three quarters of the game, Texas was ahead. It looked as if Baylor had lost the championship to its rival. About that time, a light rain began to fall. The crowds, including us, streamed out of the Baylor stadium, resigned to the fact that Texas would win.

But in the fourth quarter Baylor pulled ahead to win both the game and the championship. Today those of us on the winning side no longer remember our team's bad plays, fumbles, or incomplete passes. Instead, we remember the outcome of the game. We won!

Victory gives us a new perspective on our pain. I think the apostle John had this truth in mind when he described our ultimate "homecoming": "And He [God] shall wipe away every tear from their eyes; and there shall no longer be any death; there shall no longer be any mourning, or crying, or pain: the first things have passed away" (Revelation 21:4).

I had to remind myself of that truth last week as I conducted the funeral service for a young woman who died of cancer and left her two young daughters to spend the rest of their lives without a mother. During the last months of her illness, a tumor had eaten away most of her face and caused her to lose her eyesight. As long as I live, I will never forget the sight of the five-year-old daughter watching the casket being loaded into the hearse and sobbing uncontrollably, "Mommy, no, no, no, Mommy, *no!*" How will that little girl ever forget such a tragedy? How can the pain of that moment ever be erased from her memory? And how can John promise that one day her tears will be wiped away?

The apostle isn't saying that when we get to heaven, God will erase such experiences from our memory bank. Instead, he's proclaiming that one day, when we're reunited with our loved ones in heaven, we'll view the sting of death from a different perspective. We'll no longer view death as a victor but instead as a mere prelude to an even greater existence. The Scriptures promise that "Death is swallowed up in victory" (1 Corinthians 15:54). Again, ultimate victory changes our perspective about pain.

That truth also applies to crises we experience while living in the far country. If a job loss, bankruptcy, marital discord, or illness result in our return to God then, like Muggeridge, one day we'll view those painful experiences with satisfaction.

I've already alluded to the years I spent living in the far country. During that time, God brought three severe crises into my life. First, within a period of six months my mother was diagnosed with colon cancer and died. Second, the church I was pastoring experienced a tremendous upheaval. Two days after my mother's funeral, a church leader sat in my office and told me that he would do everything he could to remove me as pastor of the church. Finally, during that same period of time, I had a disagreement with one of my closest friends that resulted in the severance of our friendship.

After those three devastating blows, I was ready to wave the white flag of surrender. Yet as painful as those experiences were, I wouldn't trade them for anything. In fact, a strange power draws me back to the physical sites of those horrible experiences. As I've traveled back to that first church I pastored, sat in restaurants my friend and I used to frequent, and stood over my mother's grave in recent years, I still recall the pain of those moments. But, strangely, I can also feel the "particular satisfaction" Muggeridge describes, realizing that those crises were the tools God used to make me yearn for a homecoming experience.

I believe David had that kind of satisfaction in mind when he wrote of the positive value of affliction in his own life: "Before I was afflicted I went astray, but now I keep Thy word" (Psalm 119:67). David understood that without having experienced the pain of sin, he never would have enjoyed the pleasure of a homecoming.

REPENTANCE

Painful experiences alone don't guarantee a homecoming. The story of the prodigal son illustrates a second crucial step necessary to return from the far country: repentance. The word *repentance* is a much-used but seldom understood word. When we hear the word *repent,* we often conjure up images of a scraggly street preacher wearing a sandwich board announcing the end of the world. Or we may think of an emotionally charged worship service in which the audience pours to the altar in a flood of tears and public confession.

However, the word *repent (metanoeo* in Greek) is void of the sensationalism and emotion with which we associate it today. (That's reassuring to me since the most life-changing and lasting decisions I have ever made were not accompanied by a flood of tears.) Instead, the word means "to change one's mind." It describes someone headed in one direction who decides to go in the opposite direction.

Recently we were driving in a strange city on our way to spend the night with my sister and her family. Instead of turning left at the stoplight as we had been told, I made a mistake and turned right. As we drove farther and farther away from the city lights, I sensed I had made a mistake. But we males have a difficult time admitting we're wrong, especially when it comes to driving. We also suspend logic by thinking that if we travel long enough in the wrong direction, suddenly everything will turn out all right. So I kept driving farther away from my intended destination. Eventually the reality of a near-empty gas tank and two crying children ready for sleep finally convinced me that I needed to change directions.

My decision wasn't an emotional one. I don't remember sobbing uncontrollably, nor do I recall being overwhelmed with grief over my mistake. Instead, I evaluated the surrounding landscape and decided I had headed in the wrong direction. Not wanting to continue in that direction, I applied the brake, turned the steering wheel, watched for oncoming traffic, pushed the accelerator, and headed in the opposite direction. My turnaround resulted from a deliberate decision that in turn resulted in a definitive action.

Interestingly, you find the same lack of emotion in the prodigal son. Look carefully again at how he decided to journey home:

1. *He was tired of his present circumstances.* "And he was longing to fill his stomach with the pods that the swine were eating..."

2. *He experienced a moment of realization.* "But when he had come to his senses..."

3. *He decided on a course of action.* "I will get up and go to my father and say..."

4. *He acted on his decision.* "And he got up and came to his father..."

No tears, no sleepless nights, no voices from heaven, just a decision to change and the determination to act on that decision. Please understand, I'm not trying to drain our relationship with God of all emotion. But I believe that we make a tremendous mistake when we insist that emotionalism must accompany true repentance.

The denomination with which my church is affiliated has recently emphasized the need for our churches and nation to experience "genuine revival," an idea with which I certainly agree. Many of our denominational seminaries and colleges have reported "spiritual awakenings" in which thousands of students spend all day weeping, praying, and publicly confessing their sins. In one of these meetings, a professor stood at the podium and proclaimed that as wonderful as the convocation had been, the real test of its legitimacy would be in tangible changes it produced in individual lives. When the students left the auditorium would they be more loving husbands and wives, more diligent students, and more obedient Christians? Would they willingly ask forgiveness from fellow students and professors they had offended? If not, the gathering was futile.

Although many severely criticized that professor for trying to *quench* the Spirit, he understood the difference between emotionalism that usually leads nowhere and biblical repentance that always leads to a change of direction. Paul also understood the difference between emotionalism and repentance. Notice how he contrasted real repentance to emotionalism (which he labels "the sorrow of the world"): "For the sorrow that is according to the will of God produces a repentance without regret, leading to salvation; but the sorrow of the world produces death" (2 Corinthians 7:10).

True repentance should not be confused with grief

A man recently sat in my office and poured out the details of a five-year affair with another woman. His wife had overheard a phone conversation he had with his mistress and promptly filed for divorce. Faced with the prospects of losing his family, this man was overcome with grief but not repentance. We can be sorry for the pain of our sin, we can hate the consequences of our sin, and we can regret the hurt our sin has caused others without ever repenting of our sin.

Let's return to David for a moment. Some would use his life as evidence that true repentance involves emotion. Doesn't David testify of the groaning and pain that came from his sin? "My body wasted away through my groaning all day long.... My vitality was drained away as with the fever-heat of summer" (Psalm 32:3–4). Yes, but notice the phrase that precedes that emotion: "When I kept silent about my sin…" David described the remorse that arises from *unconfessed sin.* He was sorry for the family disruption, the unrelenting guilt, the loss of self-esteem, and his alienation from God. He was experiencing the "sorrow of the world" that would have eventually led to his own death. But we should never confuse that deep sorrow with genuine repentance.

True repentance does not leave a residue of regret

You may hesitate to return home from the far country because you fear you can never make up for the lost time you've spent there. I know this sounds irrational, but one reason I resisted turning my car around was that a U-turn would force me to admit that I had indeed wasted time and gasoline traveling in the wrong direction. I couldn't bear the monotony of retracing my tracks and thinking every inch of the way *"If only* I had listened to the directions." As long as I traveled in one direction—even if it was the *wrong* direction—I could feel like I was headed *somewhere.*

Let me illustrate the difficulty of repentance another way. You know how it feels to have a major project hanging over your head such as a report to write or a task to complete. Maybe you spend weeks avoiding your work by rationalizing "I have plenty of time to complete the project." But suddenly complacency is replaced with panic: "I only have _____ days to complete this project!" If you're like me, such fear only makes you procrastinate *more.* Why? Because you hate to face your own slothfulness. You realize that the moment you finally begin your project you'll haunt yourself with thoughts such as:

Why did I wait until the last minute?

Why am I putting myself through this?

If only I had begun earlier, I could have done a better job.

We all hate those "if only" thoughts, especially in our relationship with God:

If only I had said no to that temptation;
If only I had refused that promotion;
If only I had spent more time developing my relationship with God; or
If only I had listened to that counselor or friend.

We can't stand the idea of resigning ourselves to a substandard spiritual life because of our time spent in the far country. For several years I avoided restarting my daily devotional time with God out of a fear that once I began, I would be racked with regret for the years I had missed! Yes, I'll admit that my reasoning was ludicrous, but I imagine you know *exactly* what I'm talking about.

Yet Paul says that true repentance means never having to look back with regret. The moment I had my car traveling in the right direction, a surge of relief engulfed me. I never once looked into the rearview mirror, sorry that I had changed directions. My assurance that every mile I now traveled would take me closer to my destination erased any remaining regret.

We can experience the same assurance in our relationship with God. Somehow God can "make up to you for the years that the swarming locust has eaten" (Joel 2:25).

True repentance is a gift from God

Paul also reminds us that repentance—the ability to turn around—is God's gift to us. He describes repentance as "according to the will of God." No one decides to repent on his or her own. The prophet Jeremiah pleaded, "Turn thou us unto thee, O LORD, and we shall be turned" (Lamentations 5:21, KJV).

In 2 Timothy 2:24–25, Paul wrote, "The Lord's bond-servant must not be quarrelsome, but be kind to all, able to teach, patient when wronged, with gentleness correcting those who are in opposition, *if perhaps God may grant them repentance* leading to the knowledge of the truth" (emphasis mine).

After spending weeks, months, or even years in the far country, the prodigal son finally "came to his senses" (Luke 15:17). For a long time, the son had acted irrationally. It made no sense for the heir of a wealthy man and the son of a loving father to leave his home for a difficult and poverty-filled existence. Why would anyone in his right mind trade a palace for a pigpen? But as we saw in the first section of this book, materialism, pleasure, and ambition have a way of blinding us to reality.

Only through a supernatural act of God does a person ever come to his or her senses and see life clearly enough to turn around. The ability to repent is a gift from God. But He gives it only temporarily. Just because you desire to leave the far country today doesn't mean you'll possess that same desire tomorrow. The writer of Hebrews constantly warns us about hardening our hearts to God's call for repentance. He uses the Israelites' disobedience as an example:

> Therefore, just as the Holy Spirit says,
> "TODAY IF YOU HEAR HIS VOICE,
> DO NOT HARDEN YOUR HEARTS AS WHEN THEY
>   PROVOKED ME,
> AS IN THE DAY OF TRIAL IN THE WILDERNESS,
> WHERE YOUR FATHERS TRIED ME BY TESTING ME..."
>
> Take care, brethren, lest there should be in any one of you an evil, unbelieving heart, in falling away from the living God. But encourage one another day after day, as long as it is still called "Today," lest any one of you be hardened by the deceitfulness of sin. (Hebrews 3:7–9, 12–13)

Have you noticed that your possessions, your recreational pursuits, or your career don't give you the same "buzz" they once did? Do you find yourself waking up in the middle of the night with an uneasy feeling that something isn't quite right in your life? Are you realizing more and more how brief your time on earth really is? Do you find yourself thinking more about God and, more importantly, wondering what He thinks about *you?* Do you desire to make some real changes in your life?

If you answered yes to any of those questions, then you've come to a critical juncture in your life. And you haven't arrived there by yourself. The desire and ability to repent is a gift from God.

True repentance always results in definitive action

Paul wrote, "For the sorrow that is according to the will of God produces a repentance without regret, leading to salvation" (2 Corinthians 7:10). Genuine repentance leads somewhere. The word *salvation* means maturity or completion. The Corinthians' sorrow over their mistreatment of Paul led them to correct their mistake by exercising church discipline against the individual who had challenged Paul's authority as an apostle (2 Corinthians 2:6). Their definitive action caused Paul to deem their repentance as "genuine."

You see the same principle at work in the prodigal son. After he "came to his senses" and realized how bankrupt (both financially and spiritually) he was, he took some definitive action. Instead of wallowing in a sea of mud and self-pity, the son decided to do something about his situation. Jesus said, "He got up and came to his father" (Luke 15:20).

Think for a moment what the son's action involved. He had to announce to his employer that he was leaving his job, as menial as it was, for an uncertain future. He had to leave his familiar surroundings to return to a potentially hostile family. He had to admit that he had wronged his father and decide he could live as a hired servant. Yet, he was willing to do all of that because he longed to return home.

How about you? Do you sense that all is not right between you and God? Can you see how God has tried to speak to you through various crises in your life? Have you grown tired of traveling down the path that takes you farther and farther from God? Are you ready to turn around and start heading for home?

You know the old saying: A journey of a thousand miles begins with the first step. For you that first step back to your Heavenly Father might include:

- breaking off an immoral relationship;
- quitting a job that has destroyed your spiritual life;
- sacrificing your only day off to attend church;
- spending five minutes reading your Bible, even though you're bored to tears; or
- talking honestly to God about how you feel, even though you're not sure He's listening.

We've examined two of the four factors necessary for returning home: crisis and repentance. In the next chapter we'll examine the third requirement for coming home. The best thing about this requirement is that it has little to do with us and everything to do with God. If you're willing to learn from the "reproofs of life," make that U-turn, and take that first step in a new direction, you'll find a surprise awaiting...as did the prodigal son.

....

CHAPTER 12

The Waiting Father

How God's forgiveness invites us home

One of the subplots of the movie *The Color Purple* concerns a wayward nightclub singer named Sugar who works in a run-down bar by the side of a river. Sugar is the daughter of your stereotypical hellfire-and-brimstone preacher. (Is there any other kind in Hollywood?) He preaches in a church not far from the bar where his daughter performs every day.

One day Sugar is in the bar singing the song "I've Got Somethin' to Tell You," and suddenly, as if in response to her song, Sugar hears the church choir singing "God's got something to tell you!" just a few blocks away. Remembering her childhood faith and longing to return to her father, Sugar leads her small group of musicians in a processional to the church. Just as her father stands to deliver his message on the prodigal son, the doors fling open and down the aisle march Sugar and her band of sinners. "Even us sinners have soul," Sugar explains as she hugs her father.

Her father's response? A warm embrace or a flood of tears? Hardly. He stands like a statue, unmoved and unable to forgive his prodigal daughter who for years had brought disgrace to his family and his church.[1]

I believe the coldness of that fictional father illustrates why so many Christians living in the far country find it difficult to return home. Who wants to face a glowering Parent and spend the rest of his or her life paying for wayward actions? The thought of a vengeful Father is a formidable barrier to a homecoming.

One of my most vivid memories from my adolescence is the day my wife and I decided to play hooky from school. We were both honor-roll students, and I was president of our student body. We had never given our teachers or parents any trouble. But one spring day as we drove to school together, I blurted out, "Let's skip school today and do something fun." Amy reacted as if I had asked her to do drugs with me! She listed all the reasons we shouldn't do such a thing, not the least of which was the wrath we'd incur from our mothers, both of whom were high school teachers and had little patience with this kind of foolishness.

But as I continued to paint a word picture of the unending fun we'd have, Amy relented. I turned my blue Volkswagen Bug around and off we went, passing dozens of poor students who didn't know the meaning of real freedom.

"So where are we going?" Amy inquired.

"I don't know. Where do you want to go?" I deferred.

Every suggestion met with a reasonable objection: It would cost too much, we might get caught, or our parents would disapprove.

Finally, we settled on two destinations. This is so pathetic, I hate to admit it. First, we drove to my father's place of business to visit with him. He thought the whole episode was pretty funny. Then we traveled downtown to our church to hang around with our youth minister. That was it; the day was soon over. The only thing worse than our lackluster experience was the dread of returning home to face our mothers. As the afternoon turned into evening, we found it increasingly difficult to go home.

Why? We were paralyzed by the fear of our parents. How loudly would they yell? How long would we be grounded? Would they write a note to the principal excusing our absence, or would we face further punishment from him as well?

The story would have ended nicely had we found our parents standing at the front door so relieved to see us that they instantly forgave us our transgressions and welcomed us home. In reality, their wrath was worse than either one of us had imagined. Had we known what we'd face, we probably would have stayed away much longer and enjoyed ourselves more fully.

I imagine you have a similar story about suffering an angry parent's wrath. Unfortunately, such experiences color our thoughts of God. We picture God as a vengeful, unforgiving Father just waiting for an opportunity to get even. Although we may long to return home from the far country, we're reluctant to do so because we don't know what awaits us:

Will I face an angry or forgiving God?

Will I spend the rest of my life suffering the consequences of my sin?

Am I forever condemned to second-class-citizen status in God's kingdom?

A. W. Tozer writes, "What comes into our minds when we think about God is the most important thing about us."[2] If we imagine God as an unforgiving Parent who refuses to forget our sin, why would we ever want to return home? I believe this condemning image of God has prevented many unbelievers from coming to Christ and has kept many Christians, maybe even you, living in the far country. Deep down, we believe that God hates us because of our sin. And no one wants to return home to face an aggrieved and angry parent.

THE REALITY OF GOD'S FORGIVENESS

In Jesus' day the Pharisees held a strict, judgmental view of God. They taught that God despised sinners, defining *sinners* as anyone other than themselves. As a result, the masses of people ignored their message. "That's all right; truth is narrow," the Pharisees reasoned to themselves.

But then Jesus came and portrayed God in a completely different way: "My Father doesn't hate sinners, He *loves* sinners." As a result, Luke records that all the tax-gatherers—the most despised group in Jesus' day (some things never change!)—and sinners came in droves to hear Him. Upset by their failure to attract the masses and jealous of Jesus' success, the Pharisees tried to discredit His message. "And both the Pharisees and scribes began to grumble saying, 'This man receives sinners and eats with them'" (Luke 15:2).

Yet, what the Pharisees meant as an indictment was actually a compliment in Jesus' mind. "You finally have the picture! God sent Me to save, not condemn, those who are lost. God *loves* sinners and He rejoices when a sinner comes home." To illustrate this truth, which was so diametrically opposed to the religious teaching of His day, Jesus offered three illustrations that demonstrate the reality of God's love.

First, Jesus told the story of a shepherd who has one hundred sheep and loses one. How did Jesus portray the shepherd's attitude toward the lost sheep? Does the shepherd say, "Why on earth would that sheep want to leave the sheepfold? If he wants to leave that badly, let him go. He deserves whatever happens to him. I hope he gets eaten by a wolf"? Or does he say, "One sheep? Who cares? I still have ninety-nine left"?

No! Instead, the compassionate shepherd leaves his ninety-nine sheep to actively search for the lost sheep. And what is his attitude when he finds the lost sheep? Anger? Retribution? No. "And when he has found it, he lays it on his shoulders, rejoicing" (Luke 15:5).

Although most of us know nothing about shepherding, anyone who has ever owned a pet can identify with the shepherd's emotion. Perhaps you remember how, as a child, you agonized over a missing dog or cat. Over a period of hours or even days, you combed the neighborhood searching for the animal. Just when you had resigned yourself to never seeing your pet again, you noticed a familiar-looking animal, barely visible, several blocks away. You walked faster, then broke into a run, hoping against hope that the animal belonged to you. You yelled out your pet's name, and the animal stopped dead in its tracks. Recognizing your voice, your pet galloped toward you. You thought nothing of punishment, only of the joy of your reunion with something you love.

The story of the shepherd and the wayward sheep should have sufficed to prove Jesus' point. But people had the thought of an angry and unforgiving God ingrained in their minds, so Jesus used another example. Perhaps Jesus had a difficult time imagining the Pharisees as animal lovers, so he used an illustration closer to their hearts: money.

Jesus had the Pharisees ponder this question: Suppose a woman has ten silver coins and loses one of them; what is her attitude toward that lost coin? Does she reason to herself, "Well, at least I still have my other nine coins. A 10 percent loss won't kill my portfolio. I'll just guard the other nine more carefully"? No, she scours the house looking everywhere for that coin. And how does she react when she finds it? Does she throw it away in anger? Of course not! Jesus said, "And when she has found it, she calls together her friends and neighbors, saying, 'Rejoice with me, for I have found the coin which I had lost!'" (Luke 15:9).

I imagine by this time Jesus' audience was starting to get the point: You don't hate something you've lost; instead, you search for it and rejoice when you find it. But what do these two illustrations have to do with God's attitude toward sinners? Everything! "In the same way, I tell you, there is joy in the presence of the angels of God over one sinner who repents" (Luke 15:10).

When one of His children wanders away from home, God the Father doesn't passively wait for that child to return; instead, He actively pursues that lost child. And when He is reunited with His child, God responds with joy and forgiveness, not with anger and retribution. To drive that point home, Jesus used one more illustration: the story of the prodigal son.

We can't really understand this parable until we see it in the context of the previous two illustrations. All three serve to illustrate God's attitude toward sinners. God doesn't hate sinners; instead, He loves them, searches for them, and rejoices when He finds them.

Already, we've seen how the son chose to leave his home. We've discussed his existence in the far country. We've also looked at the steps involved in his decision to return: A crisis produced a change of mind that led him to take that first step home. But I think you'll agree that the most important element in the son's homecoming was not *his actions,* but *his father's attitude.* A crisis and repentance alone couldn't effect a homecoming; the father had to offer forgiveness.

RETRIBUTION VERSUS RESTORATION

Think about it. Imagine that after days of rehearsing his I'm-sorry-and-no-longer-worthy-to-be-your-son speech in the pigpen, the son finally screws up enough courage to go home. But when he finally arrives home, he finds the door locked. After banging on the door for half an hour, his mother finally comes to the door.

"Mom, I really need to talk to Dad."

"Son, I'll try, but your father is so angry over the way you treated him, I doubt he will see you. Wait here."

She disappears into the recesses of the house and after a seemingly interminable wait, she returns. "Son, I'm sorry, but today is not a good day. Maybe some other time."

"But, Mom," the boy asks incredulously, "didn't you tell him I was here?"

"Yes," she replies, trying to spare his feelings by avoiding any further details.

"Well, what did Dad say…exactly?"

"When I told him our younger son had returned, he said, 'I no longer *have* a younger son.'"

We might better relate to this kind of end to Jesus' story because it more realistically portrays how we react to those who hurt us. When we feel slighted by another person, we want to get mad *and* even.

Yesterday afternoon, a new member of our church shared with me the pain she felt from being alienated by her mother. About three months ago during a phone conversation, the mother threw a top-rate "pity party" for herself over some ailment. The daughter expressed her concern but tried to cheer up her mom by focusing on some positive aspects of her mom's life. Her mom interpreted the attempt at optimism as a lack of compassion and hung up. For the last three months, this mother has refused to speak to her daughter or to have any contact with her daughter's children, her only grandchildren.

I'll admit the mother's response is extreme, but it illustrates our tendency to inflict pain on those who hurt us. Just imagine what would have happened if, instead of merely not showing more concern for her mother's illness, the daughter had said, "Mom, I hate your guts. I wish you were dead so I could have your money. But since it doesn't appear that you're going to die any time soon, would you just give me my share of your estate so that I don't ever have to speak to you again?" That is the kind of hurt the prodigal son inflicted on his father.

Considering the son's offense, my proposed ending to the story isn't that preposterous. In fact, it's probably more realistic than the one Jesus related, given our natural tendency toward vengeance. In both endings, the son repented. But only in Jesus' finale could the son return home. What was the difference? The father's attitude. In my ending, the father reacted with anger. In Jesus' story, he responded with forgiveness.

> And he got up and came to his father. But while he was still a long way off, his father saw him, and felt compassion for him, and ran and embraced him, and kissed him. And the son said to him, "Father, I have sinned against heaven and in your sight; I am no longer worthy to be called your son." But the father said to his slaves, "Quickly bring out the best robe and put it on him, and put a ring on his hand and sandals on his feet; and bring the fattened calf, kill it, and let us eat and be merry; for this son of mine was dead, and has come to life again; he was lost and has been found." (Luke 15:20–23)

Notice several truths concerning the father's attitude toward his younger son.

The father longed for his son's return

Jesus said that even when the son was an unrecognizable dot on the horizon, his father saw him. Why? Because his father was looking for him. Every new sunrise brought the father hope that his son might return; and every new sunset inaugurated another sleepless night. The father didn't console himself with the thought, "I still have one son left; I'll pour myself into that relationship." No, he knew he could never rest until his younger boy returned home.

The father felt compassion, not anger, toward his son

First reactions are usually honest reactions. Have you ever had a conversation with one person and felt another person looking at you? When you turn and glance that other person's way, that person has a scowl on his or her face. But when that person realizes you've noticed him or her, he or she quickly replaces the scowl with a smile. And you know in your heart that the scowl, not the smile, betrays that person's true feelings toward you.

Jesus said that when the father saw his son, he had a gut reaction of compassion. In fact, the Greek word we translate as compassion means "gut reaction." The word *splancnizomai* literally means "to be moved in the bowels." (Not a particularly pleasant thought today, but in Jesus' day the bowels referred to a person's innermost being.)

The father was so overcome with love for his son that he willingly surrendered any shred of dignity and ran to meet his son. In those days, a man of dignity *never* ran. And he didn't have any "I'll meet you halfway" attitude either. The son walked toward the father; but the father *ran* to meet the son.

The father desired restoration, not retribution

The father met the son, embracing him and showering him with kisses. One can only imagine the surge of relief that engulfed the son as he realized his father's attitude.

Nevertheless, the son had to take care of business. He had probably spent weeks writing and rehearsing his speech. He might have even practiced it on the pigs:

"Dad, I know I have sinned against you and God."

"Oink."

"I realize I have no right to be called your son."

"Oink. Oink."

"However, I need a job. Would you consider hiring me as one of your slaves?"

"Oink. Oink. Oink."

But now he had no more time for rehearsals. It was time for The Speech.

As father and son walked toward the house, the father bombarded his son with questions: Where had the son been living? Had he received any of the letters his parents had written? Had he found a job? What led him to return home (carefully avoiding the subject of the money)?

As they got closer to the house, the son knew that his time was quickly running out. Soon he and his dad would face a series of awkward situations. Where would the son sleep? How would the other family members, especially his brother, react? What would the slaves think? Although the son knew things could never be the same again, he felt the need to clear the air and clarify his status. So he blurted out, "Dad, I'm sorry. I know that I have sinned against both you and God. I don't deserve to be your son, so I will work as one of your…"

But his dad quickly cut him off. He knew what his son was about to say, and he'd have none of it. All he wanted to hear were the words, "I'm sorry." No humiliating confessions. No promises of restitution. Just "I'm sorry."

The moment the father heard those words, he ordered his slaves to bring out the robe reserved for festivals. The father then slipped a ring on the son's hand—not just any ring, but a ring symbolizing his authority as his father's son. "Son, you will never be a slave in this house. You will always have authority over the slaves, because you are my son."

You may wonder what all this has to do with you. The answer is that this story tells us what kind of Father is waiting for you if you decide to return home. And knowing what awaits you can either powerfully deter you from or motivate you toward returning.

If, as the Pharisees believed, God hates you and longs to inflict His wrath upon you, why should you want to return to Him? Since you'll experience His punishment for all eternity, why begin the process early?

But Jesus Christ, the One who knows the Father more intimately than anyone else, gives us a different view of God. God doesn't hate you, He loves you. He hasn't written you off and turned his attention elsewhere; He is actively searching for you. And when you do return home, you won't face retribution but complete restoration to your previous status.

"But," you argue, "how is that possible? Doesn't the Bible teach that God hates sin? How can a holy and just God overlook my sin? How can I be sure that this picture of God as a loving and forgiving Father is accurate, not just the product of someone's imagination?"

THE BASIS FOR THE FATHER'S FORGIVENESS

You will never feel the freedom to return to God until you fully comprehend God's attitude toward your sin. And you will never be able to reconcile God's holiness with your sinfulness until you understand how He has restored you to His standard of perfection. So let's explore the Bible's teachings about sin and restoration.

God hates sin

Score one for the Pharisees; for the most part they understood God's intolerance for sin. Just consider some of the Old Testament passages that the Pharisees knew by heart:

> But your iniquities have made a separation between you and your God, and your sins have hidden His face from you, so that He does not hear. (Isaiah 59:2–3)

> God judgeth the righteous and God is angry with the wicked every day. (Psalm 7:11, KJV)

> The face of the LORD is against evildoers, to cut off the memory of them from the earth. (Psalm 34:16)

God must punish sin

Again, the Pharisees were right; since justice is a part of God's very being, He cannot simply overlook our sin. He must judge it.

You only have I known among all the families of the earth; therefore, I will punish you for all your iniquities. (Amos 3:2, KJV)

He sent upon them His burning anger, fury, and indignation, and trouble, a band of destroying angels. He leveled a path for His anger; He did not spare their soul from death, but gave over their life to the plague. (Psalm 78:49–50)

A jealous and avenging God is the LORD; the LORD is avenging and wrathful. The LORD takes vengeance on His adversaries, and He reserves wrath for His enemies. The LORD is slow to anger and great in power, and the LORD will by no means leave the guilty unpunished. (Nahum 1:2–3)

Jesus Christ paid the penalty for our sin

A few days ago, I discussed the content of this chapter with motivational speaker Jay Strack. In response to what I shared, Jay told me of an experience he had in Rome a number of years ago. While touring the Vatican, Jay ventured off by himself, eventually traveling down a staircase to a room containing some of the Vatican's most treasured works of art. Jay found his attention immediately drawn to a painting of the prodigal son he had never seen before. In the picture, the father didn't just embrace his returning son; the father also protected his son from the angry mob of citizens who felt that the son should receive punishment for his actions. In the painting, the father shielded his son from sticks and rocks thrown by the crowd. Jay observed, "What impressed me was that the father had already suffered the rejection of his son, and now he was willing to suffer the anger of the crowd meant for his son."

That is a beautiful illustration of what Jesus Christ has done for us. Even though we've rejected God, Christ willingly endured the punishment we deserve. Jesus didn't come to earth primarily to model ethical behavior or to teach us great truths about God; He came first and foremost to suffer the punishment for our sin. In some inexplicable way, when Jesus hung on that cross two thousand years ago He incurred the full wrath of God for our sin.

The Pharisees missed this central truth about Jesus, and it's difficult to understand why. For hundreds of years, the Old Testament prophets had looked forward to the coming of God's Son who would save us from our sins. Seven hundred years before Christ's birth, Isaiah the prophet foretold of His death:

> Surely our griefs He Himself bore, and our sorrows He carried; yet we ourselves esteemed Him stricken, smitten of God, and afflicted. But He was pierced through for our transgressions, He was crushed for our iniquities; the chastening for our well-being fell upon Him, and by His scourging we are healed. All of us like sheep have gone astray, each of us has turned to his own way; but the LORD has caused the iniquity of us all to fall on Him. (Isaiah 53:4–6)

Please note that God hasn't simply overlooked our mistakes. God Himself said such a thing is impossible: "I will not acquit the guilty" (Exodus 23:7). Instead, God poured out His anger on His own Son, rather than on us. As Jesus suffered on the cross, He felt the full brunt of God's rage. In those hours at Calvary, Jesus Christ experienced Hell—separation from God—for you and me. And because of His experience, we need no longer fear God's wrath.

Perhaps this illustration will help you understand how Christ's death ensures that you never need to dread God's judgment. You may remember from nature that a worker bee can sting only once in its lifetime. It has a needle-sharp stinger equipped with little barbs along its sides like the quills of a porcupine. When the bee inserts its stinger, the stinger goes in to stay. Thus the only way the bee can free itself from its victim is to tear itself from the stinger, leaving the stinger in the victim. The bee without a stinger can still buzz and scare people for a while, but it can no longer harm another person.

When Jesus Christ died on the cross, He suffered the "sting" of God's judgment. And because of His experience, we no longer have to fear God's judgment. God's wrath can sting only once. Paul had this truth in mind when he wrote, "O death, where is your victory? O death, where is your sting? The sting of death is sin, and the power of sin is the law; but thanks be to God, who gives us the victory through our Lord Jesus Christ" (1 Corinthians 15:55–57).

However, countless passages in the Bible make it clear that this deliverance from God's future judgment isn't for everyone. Instead, it's reserved for those who trust in Christ's ability to save them from God's judgment. Jesus explained it simply enough for even a child to understand: "For God so loved the world, that He gave His only begotten Son, that whoever believes in Him should not perish, but have eternal life" (John 3:16).

You've probably heard this truth since childhood, and I hope you can point to a time in your life when you acknowledged your sin to God and placed your faith in Jesus Christ. If so, you *know* that at that time God forgave you of all of your sins.

But perhaps much has happened in your life since that experience many years ago: an affair, a failed marriage, an addiction, an unethical business deal, a lapse of faith, or maybe just a slow drift away from God. For you the question is, "What does God think about me right *now*? Is He disappointed with me? Is He angry with me? If I do return home, will He answer the door?"

THE EXTENT OF GOD'S FORGIVENESS

You'll never grasp God's present attitude toward you until you understand the extent of God's forgiveness of your sins. I know of no better verse in the Bible that explains the totality of God's forgiveness than Colossians 2:13–14: "And when you were dead in your transgressions and the uncircumcision of your flesh, He made you alive together with Him, having forgiven us all our transgressions, having canceled out the certificate of debt consisting of decrees against us and which was hostile to us; and He has taken it out of the way, having nailed it to the cross." These verses answer two important questions about God's forgiveness.

Which of my sins has God forgiven?

To me, the best word in these two verses is the little word *all*. God has forgiven us for *all* our sins. Most of us find that concept difficult to accept. We mistakenly think that God is created in our image instead of our being created in His. Thus, we assume that His ability to forgive is as limited as ours.

And just how limited is our ability to forgive? We find it relatively easy to overlook people's minor offenses: "I forgive you for not smiling at me yesterday," or "I will overlook your forgetting our anniversary—this time at least!" But we find it much more difficult to overlook major offenses: a slanderous comment, an affair, violence, or dishonesty.

Not God. The Bible says that because of Christ's death for us, God's forgiveness is total, not partial. God doesn't forgive just the little sins; He forgives the big ones as well. Isn't it interesting that Paul uses the word *us* instead of *you* when describing the object of God's forgiveness? I believe that the apostle Paul placed special importance on the knowledge that God's forgiveness covers all of our sins. Before he became a Christian, Paul had been guilty of blasphemy, torture, and murder, yet God's forgiveness sufficiently covered all those offenses. Listen to Paul's testimony of God's amazing grace:

> …I was formerly a blasphemer and a persecutor and a violent aggressor.
> And yet I was shown mercy, because I acted ignorantly in unbelief; and
> the grace of our Lord was more than abundant, with the faith and love
> which are found in Christ Jesus. It is a trustworthy statement, deserving
> full acceptance, that Christ Jesus came into the world to save sinners,
> among whom I am foremost of all (1 Timothy 1:13–15).

Maybe you've remained in the far country for so long because you've found it difficult to believe that God could really forgive you of *all* your sins. To help you apply the truth of God's complete forgiveness, on a separate sheet of paper make a list of your sins that you have trouble believing that God could forgive—sins that could be inserted into Colossians 2:13–14.

And when I was dead in *my* transgressions and the uncircumcision
of *my* flesh, He made *me* alive together with Him, having forgiven
me of _____.

Now, take a pen and draw a single line through each of the sins you listed,
and to the side write the word *forgiven*. You'll never feel the freedom to return
to your Heavenly Father until you understand His complete forgiveness.

What has God done with my sin?

A number of years ago I got involved in a terrible real-estate deal. A developer
and a savings and loan company duped me into buying a damaged building
that I could never resell. My attorney advised me to walk away from the loan
since the savings and loan corporation had been involved in the fraud. As a
result, the savings and loan sued me for back payments. Finally, a court ruled
in my favor, releasing me from the debt. In the court's written ruling was a
phrase I did not understand: "with prejudice." My attorney explained that
those words meant that never again would the court reexamine this case. I
never needed to fear that at some future date my opponents would again
dredge up this case and come knocking on my door for money. The court
had settled the matter once and for all.

Paul employs that same imagery in describing God's forgiveness. The
apostle explains that God has "canceled out the certificate of debt." In Paul's
day, the "certificate of debt" was much like the mortgage note I signed with
the savings and loan company. It was an IOU that a debtor would write in
his own handwriting acknowledging his indebtedness. For example:

I, Robert Jeffress, owe the Colossians Savings and Loan the sum of
30 million denarii.

Paul says we're in debt to God because of our sins. In Romans 6:23 Paul
writes "For the wages of sin is death..." We owe God for the sins we've
committed.

But when we become Christians, God cancels our certificates of debt.

The Greek word translated "canceled out" means to "wipe away." In Paul's day, official documents were written on expensive paper or animal hide. The acid-free ink used to write a note wouldn't bite into the surface of the paper or hide but could be easily erased and the paper used again. (And you thought recycling was a new idea!)

The moment you become a Christian, God takes the list of all of your sins, and He doesn't merely draw a line through them as you did a moment ago, but He actually wipes them away. We never have to worry that at some future time God will dredge up our sins for further review. Why? No record of them remains. The prophet Micah had this truth in mind when he wrote: "...Thou wilt cast all their sins into the depths of the sea" (Micah 7:19).

"Well, that may be true about my sins *before* I became a Christian, but what about those sins I've committed *since* becoming a Christian?" Let me ask you a question. When Christ died for your sins two thousand years ago, which sins did He die for? Remember, at that time all of your sins would happen in the future. When Paul affirms that God has forgiven us of all of our sins, he means *all* sins—past, present, and future.

Several years ago *Moody Magazine* ran an article I wrote about the subject of "Guilt-Free Prayer" in which I listed seven myths about prayer that keep us from praying. One of those myths is "God will not answer my prayers if there is any unconfessed sin in my life." We create a formidable barrier to prayer when we adhere to the mistaken notion that we must be perfect before God will hear us. I further explained the truth we have just seen concerning the extent of God's forgiveness. God has *already* forgiven us of all of our sins. When we sin as Christians, God doesn't suddenly change our status from forgiven to guilty until we confess our transgressions. Such erroneous teaching negates the results of Christ's death. If my sin as a Christian erects a barrier between my Father and me, then He didn't fully forgive me of my sins two thousand years ago, and He hasn't completely wiped my slate clean.

The reaction from my article was extreme. The next issue of the magazine contained a number of letters to the editor about the article, some expressing appreciation and others labeling me a heretic. Some of the critical letters quoted passages from the Bible that spoke of the importance of Christians acknowledging their sin to God. No argument here. I fully agree that as Christians we need to confess and repent of our sins. But we confess our sins not to change God's attitude toward us but to change our attitudes toward God.

This reminds me of the story of the couple married for twenty-five years. On the way to their anniversary dinner, the wife began to complain to her husband (who was driving the car), "Herbert, when we first started dating we always used to sit next to one another in the car. Now look at the distance between us. You're way over there, and I'm over here."

Herbert replied, "Dear, *I* haven't moved."

No matter what first enticed you to leave God and regardless of the length of time you've remained in the far country, He has not moved. Through the death of His Son, God has completely erased the debt of your sin. And now He stands watching, waiting, and longing for your return.

No feeling compares to the relief that comes from God's forgiveness. David expressed that relief this way: "Oh, what joy for those whose rebellion is forgiven, whose sin is put out of sight! Yes, what joy for those whose record the LORD has cleared of sin, whose lives are lived in complete honesty" (Psalm 32:1–2, NLT).

Like David, you may have experienced the complete cycle of wandering: crisis, repentance, and forgiveness. Now you're back home and determined to never drift again. Although you may sincerely wish this, there is one seldom-mentioned truth about coming home that makes it difficult to maintain your resolve: There's always a "morning after." In the next chapter we'll explore the fourth requirement necessary for a genuine homecoming experience: perseverance.

....

The Morning After

A prescription for perseverance

What do these events have in common?

Mondays.

The day after your summer vacation ends.

December 26.

The morning following your fortieth birthday party.

They all signal the end of a celebration. We usually find the morning after a celebration difficult, not only because it means the cessation of fun, but it also signals the resumption of routine.

Probably the greatest celebration I've ever enjoyed was the night of my fortieth birthday party. My church pulled out all the stops for a gala event. One hundred of my family members and closest friends from out of town gathered for a reception prior to the evening worship service. During the service, the choir and orchestra performed my favorite hymns. Then, to climax the event, my lifelong pastor and mentor Dr. W. A. Criswell delivered the message. As I surveyed the filled sanctuary and looked into the eyes of those people I love the most, I remember thinking, "Life doesn't get any better than this." At the end of the service, the organist started to play a familiar funeral dirge, the doors to the sanctuary swung open, and six hooded "executioners" marched solemnly down the aisle and escorted me into the balloon-filled gymnasium for a "roast" attended by fifteen hundred of my friends and parishioners. What a party!

The next morning, I wandered into the gymnasium littered with confetti and paper plates from the previous night's celebration. The left side of the "Happy Birthday, Pastor" banner had detached from the wall. The helium balloons had started to sag. The only other person in the room was a janitor shaking his head as he attempted to clear the debris. A room that just twelve hours earlier had been a scene of jubilation was now a truly depressing sight. My friends and family members had departed, my church members had returned to work in the real world, my "to do" pile loomed higher than ever. And if those thoughts weren't depressing enough, I was one year closer to death!

Perhaps the prodigal son felt some of these same emotions the morning after his homecoming party. The celebration his father had hosted the night before was one he would never forget. The dad carefully orchestrated every detail of the affair; when the son returned, the father ordered: "Quickly bring out the best robe and put it on him, and put a ring on his hand and sandals on his feet; and bring the fattened calf, kill it, and let us eat and be merry; for this son of mine was dead, and has come to life again; he was lost, and has been found." And they began to be merry (Luke 15:22–24).

Later in the story, we discover that this celebration was no small family gathering but involved numerous guests and included music and even dancing—the only element my Baptist congregation excluded from my party! The son's homecoming certainly warranted a huge celebration. Understandably, Jesus chose to end the story on a high note. As Luke 15 fades to black, the orchestra still plays and the guests still party.

But what about the next morning? I've never heard anyone speculate on the scene around the prodigal's house the morning after the homecoming. I imagine that everyone slept a little late that morning, exhausted from the previous night's festivities and emotionally drained from the events surrounding the son's reconciliation with his father. What do you suppose the son thought of as he lay in bed trying to summon the strength to begin the day's activities? I believe he must have experienced a tremendous letdown as he realized that he was about to resume the same life that had caused him to leave home in the first place. Think about it for a moment; not all that much had changed since the day he had departed from home.

He was still under his father's authority. The prodigal son's homecoming did not absolve him of his daily household responsibilities. After the "grace period" of the first day's reentry into the family, the father probably had plenty of tasks for his younger son. Gone were the days of hedonism that had characterized the son's existence for the last several months or even years.

He still had to contend with an obnoxious older brother. The older brother was neither sorry to see his sibling leave nor thrilled to see him return. The older brother's expression of anger at the younger son's homecoming celebration was nothing new. For years these two had hated one another. The younger son resented his brother always taking their dad's side in every disagreement. The older brother resented the way his father overlooked the younger son's rebellion.

Being a firstborn child myself, I can easily sympathize with the older brother's emotions. We firstborns are often compliant and obedient children. We want to please our parents. It doesn't seem fair to us that a rebellious brother or sister should receive the same treatment as we do, much less *better* treatment. "Dad, I've always obeyed you, and you've never thrown a party for me. Why are you honoring a son who has wasted your money on prostitutes and booze?" He had a point.

At the end of the story, the father stands outside the house with the older son trying to persuade him to join the celebration. Given the intense enmity between the two brothers, I doubt the father's "I love you both equally" speech did much good. I imagine the younger son had to endure the sarcastic comments of his brother for the rest of his life.

He still had a taste for sin. As we saw earlier, life in the far country is not all pain. I imagine that from time to time the younger son remembered the fun he had enjoyed: the parties, the women, the freedom. If he were really honest with himself, he missed that part of his life. As he listened to his father bark orders at the breakfast table every morning and endured the taunts of his older brother, he probably thought, "I came home for *this?*"

PERSEVERING PAST THE CRISIS

I could have ended this book with the last chapter. What better way to close our journey than by encouraging you that, regardless of whether you've allowed money, pleasure, or ambition to entice you from God, if you take that first step home, you'll find a forgiving Father ready to embrace you.

Yet, such an ending would have been a dishonest one. For there's always a *morning after* a homecoming experience. No matter how sincere and firm our resolve to renew our relationship with God, we'll always feel the pull toward our old ways of living. C. S. Lewis expresses it this way in his book *The Problem of Pain:*

> I am progressing along the path of life in my ordinary, contentedly fallen and godless condition, absorbed in a merry meeting with my friends for the morrow or a bit of work that tickles my vanity today, a holiday or a new book, when suddenly a stab of abdominal pain that threatens serious disease, or a headline in the newspapers that threatens us all with destruction, sends this whole pack of cards tumbling down.
>
> At first I am overwhelmed, and all my little happinesses look like broken toys. Then, slowly and reluctantly, bit by bit, I try to bring myself into the frame of mind that I should be in at all times. I remind myself that all these toys were never intended to possess my heart, that my true good is in another world and my only real treasure is Christ. And perhaps, by God's grace, I succeed, and for a day or two become a creature consciously dependent on God and drawing its strength from the right sources. But the moment the threat is withdrawn, my whole nature leaps back to the toys.[1]

If you were motivated to purchase and read this book, I imagine you can identify with Lewis' words. For years you've probably traveled down a path that has led you further and further from God. Slowly, almost imperceptibly, your very real need to earn a living has turned into an obsession with money, your need for periodic relaxation has turned into an insatiable desire for pleasure, or your desire to maximize your God-given abilities has evolved into blind ambition. The Enemy successfully encouraged you to deny, not the existence of God, but your *need* for God.

Then one day a cancer scare, a broken marriage, a financial setback, or a rebellious child grabs your attention. You realize that in fact you *do* need God. And so as sincerely as you know how, you admit your mistakes to God, plead for His forgiveness, and resolve to make some life changes that may include:

- Returning to a marriage that long ago lost its vitality;
- Giving up an addiction that has destroyed everything in your life;
- Ending an illicit affair that has overwhelmed you with guilt;
- Resigning from a job that has constantly tempted you into work-aholism;
- Devoting more time and energy to your children; or
- Committing to spend time with God daily.

Your commitment is sincere but short-lived. When the fog lifts, the storm passes, and your crisis ceases, you're inclined to "leap back to the toys" as Lewis says. "Prone to wander, Lord I feel it, prone to leave the God I love." For this reason, we need to understand the fourth requirement for a genuine, lasting homecoming experience: perseverance.

When Jerry and Paula met, they had both just ended long-term relationships. Within three months of their first date, they were married. Their ten-year union had produced three children, all of whom were dedicated Christians. Then one afternoon, Jerry confessed to me that he no longer loved his wife, and he wanted a divorce. He said that after the first month of their marriage, he had known he had made a mistake and wanted to leave.

But his Christian beliefs and later his children motivated him to stick it out. But now he realized he wasn't getting any younger nor was his marriage getting any better. And besides, there was this girl in his office who…(you know the rest of the story).

After several hours of pleading, arguing, and rebuking, I could see that Jerry intended to dissolve his marriage. His wife was devastated and his children heartbroken over the loss of husband and father. But they wouldn't give up. They prayed daily that God would open Jerry's spiritual eyes to the reality of his sin.

A few months later, Jerry came to see me again. Health problems, financial difficulties, and overwhelming guilt had conspired to bring Jerry back to his family. "Yesterday I told God how sorry I was and last night I begged for my family's forgiveness. Pastor, I wanted you to be the first to know that I am going back home." I led a prayer of thanksgiving for him, then reminded him of some of the issues that still needed resolution and some of the obstacles he would face. He nodded in agreement.

Being a close-knit congregation, many in our church knew the details of Jerry and Paula's marriage. Like me, they grieved over the separation and the impact it had on the children. And they were also thrilled when they heard that the marriage had been salvaged. The next Sunday, Jerry and Paula strolled through the church halls holding hands. People patted them on the back and offered their congratulations. God had performed a miracle!

However, every time I saw Jerry I sensed a cloud over his faith. When together, Paula seemed to smile much more than Jerry. Several months later, Jerry moved out again and filed for divorce. After the final separation, Jerry visited me one last time. "What happened?" I wanted to know. "Pastor, when I went back home everything was great the first few months. Although we were all walking on eggshells, it was just good to be back with my family. But within a few days I knew that nothing had really changed. We fell back into the same arguments, but this time they were worse because Paula kept reminding me what a louse I was for having left my family. The only place worse than home was the church. People smiled at me, but I felt their judgmental spirits. I knew that they would never look at me the same way again. Staying in that marriage just wasn't worth the hassle."

HOW TO STAY HOME ONCE YOU'VE COME HOME

I'm convinced that one reason returning prodigals don't stay home is that no one shoots straight with them about the true nature of the "morning after." It's difficult! But it's also worth the effort it takes to rebuild a severed relationship with God. Let me offer you four invaluable suggestions for persevering in obedience long after the homecoming celebration has ended.

Maintain realistic expectations

The greatest source of conflict in any relationship is unrealistic and, therefore, unmet expectations. For example, the relationship between a pastor and a church can suffer from unrealistic expectations. The pastor expects church members to always affirm him or her and never voice a critical comment. The church expects the pastor to be on call twenty-four hours a day, seven days a week. Such unrealistic expectations from both parties produce conflict.

Unrealistic expectations can also hinder a Christian's relationship with God. Let me warn you of several expectations to guard against.

First, *don't expect your sinful desires to evaporate.* Whatever Satan has used to lure you from God—money, pleasure, or ambition—you'll probably find tempting for the rest of your life. You may not find this comforting news, but it's the truth.

Remember Joseph's story? Potiphar, a powerful Egyptian, put Joseph in charge of running his household. The only problem was that Mrs. Potiphar lusted for Joseph. Winks, suggestive comments, and lingering glances all signaled what she really wanted. However, one day she got tired of playing games and decided to get down to business. When she and Joseph were alone she said, "Lie with me" (a tepid English translation of the Hebrew which reads, "Let's party!"). But Joseph refused by saying, "How then could I do this great evil, and sin against God?" (Genesis 39:9). Joseph made a once-for-all decision that he would not commit adultery. End of story, right? Wrong.

Don't think that just because you've said no to sin once that you'll never have to deal with it again. The next verse reads, "And it came about as she spoke to Joseph *day after day,* that he did not listen to her to lie beside her, or be with her (Genesis 39:10, emphasis mine).

We like to think we can make a one-time decision that will forever deliver us from an addiction, an illicit relationship, greed, or some other barrier to our relationship with God. Unfortunately, life doesn't work that way. Sin *never* loses its appeal.

Second, *don't expect instant forgiveness from others.* In the prodigal son's story, the older brother represents the attitude of the Pharisees who, unlike God the Father, didn't rejoice in a sinner's homecoming; they *resented* it! "It isn't fair," they'd argue, "that someone who has enjoyed all the fun of the far country can be instantly restored to a relationship with God."

Regardless of what the history books tell you, this sect of Jews didn't die out in the first century. Pharisees are alive, well, and active today. Sure, they may be first in line to welcome you back into the church and assure you of their prayers. But never doubt that they'll also be the first to dredge up your transgressions whenever it suits their purposes.

Yet, not everyone who refuses to instantly forgive you of your transgression deserves the "Pharisee" label. Often those closest to you have the most difficulty letting go of your offenses because they're the ones you've most deeply wounded.

I love the story about the man who lamented an argument he had with his wife. "I just hate fighting with my wife. Every time we have a disagreement, she gets historical."

"You mean hysterical," the friend corrected.

"No," he insisted, "I mean historical. Every time we argue she drags up everything from the past and holds it against me!"[2]

If your years in the far country have deeply wounded your spouse, parents, or children, don't become angry or discouraged when they find it difficult to let go of the hurt you inflicted upon them. It will take both time and consistency in your behavior to earn their trust again.

May I change audiences for a moment and say a word to those of you attempting to welcome a prodigal back home? Months and maybe even years of anxiety, hurt, and humiliation may make it difficult for you to forgive the other person's offenses. It doesn't seem fair or even possible that a simple "I'm sorry" should erase all the pain of the past. How can you forgive someone instantly and completely? Only by remembering the forgiveness God has extended to *you*.

Jesus once told a fascinating story about a king who demanded that a slave pay back the debt he owed. The slave owed the king about $5 billion in today's currency. Unable to pay and knowing that he faced certain death, the slave begged for mercy. The king, moved with compassion, forgave the slave of *all* his debt.

As the suddenly debt-free slave walked out of the palace, he remembered that a fellow slave owed him some money as well, about sixteen dollars in today's currency. When he demanded repayment, his friend begged for mercy. But the slave refused to extend the same forgiveness he had just experienced and had his friend imprisoned.

When the king heard what had happened, he was furious. "How could you refuse to forgive a sixteen-dollar debt when I have just forgiven you a five-billion-dollar debt?" the king demanded. The king then ordered the slave imprisoned until he repaid the entire debt.

Jesus closes this parable of forgiveness by declaring, "So shall My heavenly Father also do to you, if each of you does not forgive his brother from your heart" (Matthew 18:35).

The point of the story is obvious. Why should we forgive those who have wronged us? Not because they deserve our forgiveness, but because of the forgiveness God has extended to us. No matter how severely someone has wronged you, that offense is insignificant compared to the sin you've committed against God, just as a sixteen-dollar debt is insignificant compared to a five-billion-dollar one. As Paul wrote, "And be kind to one another, tender-hearted, forgiving each other, *just as* God in Christ also has forgiven you" (Ephesians 4:32, emphasis mine).

Third, if you're a returning prodigal *don't expect all the consequences of your mistakes to disappear.* Yes, God completely erases our sin. We never have to fear that one day God will become *historical* with us and dredge up all our past mistakes. As Micah the prophet says, God "wilt cast all their sins into the depths of the sea" (Micah 7:19).

Nevertheless, we reap the consequences of living in the far country, consequences that impact us for the rest of our lives. Think about the prodigal son for a moment. His time in the far country cost him his share of his father's estate. We'd like to think that just *maybe* the father would have been so glad that his son returned that he'd say, "Son, don't worry about the wealth you lost. I'm calling my attorney today, and I'm going to draw up a new will so that you'll still receive your portion of my estate when I die." But the father didn't respond that way. Why? Because such an action would have been unfair to the older son, and it would have violated the law of the day that prescribed that two-thirds of a father's estate belonged to the oldest son.

Similarly, God's forgiveness must be balanced with His universal law that says "whatever a man sows, this he will also reap" (Galatians 6:7). Randy Alcorn has illustrated this law in an article entitled "Consequences of a Moral Tumble." In that article, Randy states that whenever he is tempted with sexual sin, he reflects on the consequences of immoral activity. Randy doesn't doubt God's ability to forgive, but neither does he doubt the indelible impression immorality will make on his life. What are the lasting consequences of immorality?

> Grieving the Lord who redeemed me…
> Inflicting untold hurt on…your best friend and loyal wife…losing [her] respect and trust…
> Hurting my beloved daughters…
> Destroying my example and credibility with my children, and

nullifying both present and future efforts to teach them to obey God...

Causing shame to my family...

Creating a form of guilt awfully hard to shake. Even though God would forgive me, would I forgive myself?

Forming memories and flashbacks that could plague future intimacy with my wife...

Wasting years of ministry training and experience for a long time, maybe permanently...

Undermining the faithful example and hard work of other Christians in our community...

Bringing great pleasure to Satan, the enemy of God and all that is good...

Possibly bearing the physical consequences of such diseases as gonorrhea, syphilis, chlamydia, herpes, and AIDS; perhaps infecting [my wife] or, in the case of AIDS, even causing her death...

Possibly causing pregnancy, with the personal and financial implications, including a lifelong reminder of my sins...

Causing shame and hurt to my friends, especially those I've led to Christ and discipled...[3]

As the prodigal son can testify—as well as countless others throughout history—life in the far country can be very expensive. Some might argue that experiencing the consequences of sin contradicts God's love and forgiveness. After all, if God truly loves and forgives us, why doesn't He erase sin's sting temporally as well as eternally? The answer lies in God's love for us. If we didn't experience the consequences that accompany sin, we'd continually wander from home. Having to experience sin's consequences powerfully motivates us to stay close to our Father.

In the geographical area in which I minister, natural gas production is a major industry. When we think of natural gas, we think of the terrible odor it produces. But in its pure state, natural gas is practically odorless.

Distributors chemically add the horrible stench. Why? Because natural gas is poisonous; a leak in your home can incapacitate and even kill you and your family. The odor serves as a warning that something is wrong.

In the same way, God sometimes insists that we smell the stench and feel the pain of our sin to keep us close to home. David understood this truth. Even though he had experienced God's overwhelming forgiveness for his adultery with Bathsheba and murder of Uriah, he never resented experiencing the consequences of his sin. He understood that such consequences kept him tethered to his Father. Thus he wrote, "Before I was afflicted I went astray, but now I keep Thy word" (Psalm 119:67).

That truth closely relates to a second suggestion for remaining at home.

Regularly reflect upon the pain of the past

A woman visiting Switzerland came upon a sheepfold one day. She saw dozens of sheep seated on the ground, surrounding the shepherd. But in the corner lay a single sheep in a pile of straw, obviously suffering great pain. Upon further inspection she noticed that the sheep's leg was broken. She asked the shepherd what had happened. "I broke it myself," he responded.

Sensing her surprise, the shepherd elaborated. "Of all the sheep in my flock, this one was the most wayward. It would not obey my voice and often wandered away from the flock. On several occasions it wandered to the edge of a perilous cliff. Not only that, but it was starting to lead other sheep astray as well. I knew I had no choice, so I broke its leg.

"At first, the sheep was resentful. When I would attempt to feed it, it nearly bit my hand off. But after a few days it became submissive and obedient. Today, no sheep hears my voice so quickly, nor follows more closely."[4]

What kept the sheep close to the shepherd? The memory of the shepherd's discipline. Whenever that sheep was tempted to leave the fold, it remembered the terror of watching the shepherd crush its leg and the agonizing pain that refused to go away.

In the same way, remembering the pain of life in the far country can motivate us to remain home. Why? Most of us have selective memories. We have a natural tendency to remember the pleasure and forget the pain of our time in the far country. No doubt the prodigal son daydreamed at times about the freedom and pleasure he once enjoyed, especially when his father acted unreasonably or his brother antagonized him unnecessarily. I believe that the prodigal remained under his father's roof only by balancing his memories of pleasure with his memories of the pigpen.

The same is true for us. To remain close to our Father, we must regularly recall…

- The paralyzing fear that our mate would find out about the affair;
- The humiliation of having our addiction discovered;
- The constant worry that our financial "house of cards" would suddenly collapse;
- The despair of hearing our lifelong mate declare "I'm leaving";
- The drudgery of living a life without purpose; or
- The fear of dying without ever having reconciled with God.

For myself, I've discovered I can easily remember the pain of the past if I keep a spiritual journal. I write in my spiritual journal several times a week, recording significant events in my life and, more importantly, what God teaches me through those events. Since no one else will ever read these journals (I hope), I can afford to be brutally honest about my feelings and my doubts.

Thankfully, I continued to write in my journal during my stint in the far country. As I reread my entries from those years, two emotions overwhelm me: (1) gratitude for God's mercy in delivering me from that time in my life, and (2) determination *never* to repeat those mistakes.

If you're a returning prodigal who hasn't kept a journal during your time in the far country, let me encourage you to take an hour or two and honestly record what that time of your life was like. Then reread your summary regularly.

You may wonder if this is really a healthy activity. I assure you that it's not only profitable, it's also biblical. As Israel stood on the brink of entering the Promised Land, God commanded his prodigal nation to remember the time they spent as slaves in Egypt and their forty years wandering in the wilderness because of their disobedience:

> And you shall remember that you were a slave in the land of Egypt, and the LORD your God brought you out of there by a mighty hand and by an outstretched arm. (Deuteronomy 5:15)

> And you shall remember that you were a slave in Egypt, and you shall be careful to observe these statutes. (Deuteronomy 16:12)

> Remember the days of old, consider the years of all generations. (Deuteronomy 32:7)

Had the Israelites faithfully reflected on God's discipline in the past, they probably wouldn't have rebelled once they entered the Promised Land.

Keep the communication lines open

Next to unrealistic expectations, lack of communication is the greatest threat to healthy relationships. For example, I've noticed that whenever we miss a church staff meeting, relationships between employees become increasingly strained. Tempers flair more easily and disagreements become more petty. Why? The lack of regular communication allows ill feelings to fester and erroneous assumptions to endure.

The same is true in a family. If family members have no regular time for talking honestly with one another or for coordinating their schedules, misunderstanding and resentment will surely divide the family. I think that lack of communication probably contributed to the younger son's departure from home. Maybe the father was negligent in communicating his unconditional love for his son. As a result, the son wrongly assumed that his father had more interest in his work or his older brother than in him.

Regular communication with our Heavenly Father can also keep us from misunderstandings and wrong assumptions that might lead us back into the far country. Unfortunately, many of us pastors and authors have turned prayer and Bible study into legalistic rituals rather than opportunities for honest communication with our Father. For example, we encourage *formula* praying. "Make sure you balance your praying with adoration, confession, thanksgiving, along with your supplications. And by the way, don't ask God for too many selfish requests. It's better to ask Him for the things He wants instead of the things you want."

No wonder people think of prayer as a duty rather than a privilege! Such teaching wrings all the honesty and spontaneity from prayer. In contrast, the Bible encourages open and honest communication with God. As John Bunyan wrote, "Prayer is a sincere, sensible, affectionate pouring out of the heart or soul to God."

While prayer allows us to talk honestly with God, Bible study allows God to talk honestly with *us*. Yet, once again, we've turned a privilege into a requirement. Our "Read through the Bible in a Year" schedules and "A Chapter a Day Keeps the Devil Away" philosophies subtly communicate that Bible study is an end in itself rather than a means to an end. As a former professor of mine used to say, "The question is not how many times have you been through the Bible, but how many times has the Bible been through *you?*"

I often remind people that the Bible took sixteen hundred years to write, so why try to race through it in a year? Instead, if you really want to hear God speak to you through His Word, let me make a few practical suggestions.

Use a translation of the Bible that speaks to you. If you can understand the King James Version, more power to you. But many people have found that modern translations and paraphrases such as the New International Version or the New Living Bible are more helpful in trying to understand the Bible. Use the translation that you find easiest to understand.

Concern yourself more with consistency than with quantity. Spending even *a little* time each day reading God's Word is better than spending no time at all. Unfortunately, when you chain yourself to a systematic Bible-reading program such as reading three chapters a day, you can easily fall into an all-or-nothing mentality. If a change in your schedule doesn't allow you to read your assigned portion of Scripture for a day, you'll probably forego any Bible reading that day and pledge to make it up the next day. Soon, you find yourself so hopelessly behind that you give up Bible study for weeks or even months.

Instead, make a goal of reading something from God's Word every day. Some days your schedule may permit you to read an entire book of the Bible; other days you may be able to read only a paragraph or a verse. Whatever your time allows is okay; just provide God an opportunity to speak to you through His Word every day.

Make application the goal of your Bible study. As someone has said, "God did not give us the Bible to make us smarter sinners!" The goal of Bible study isn't increased knowledge but increased obedience. Never conclude your reading of God's Word without developing at least one specific step of action for applying what you've just read.[5]

Remember the Father's love

Perhaps the greatest benefit of regular Bible reading is that it not only reminds us of our Father's expectations of us but also His *feelings for us.* In spite of our wandering, doubts, rebellion, and inconsistencies, God's love for us never wavers. "If we are faithless, He remains faithful" the apostle Paul declared in 2 Timothy 2:13. I don't know about you, but I need to hear that *often.*

Robert Schuller tells the story of a little boy who made a miniature sailboat. After he spent months building the little red boat, he took it to a pond to test it. As he placed it in the water, the wind caught the boat's sail and carried it far beyond the boy's reach. The boy was heartbroken over the loss of that boat upon which he had labored so diligently.

Several days later as he was walking down the street, the boy noticed his little red boat for sale in the display window of a toy store. He asked the store owner for the boat, explaining that it really belonged to him. But the owner refused to return it, arguing that he had bought it from someone else. If the boy wanted it, it would cost him fourteen dollars.

The boy reached into his pocket, pulled out the money, and purchased the boat. Walking toward home and clutching the boat to his chest, the boy said, "You're my boat twice now. Once, because I made you, and now because I bought you."

Never forget that regardless of where you are in life now or where you've been in the past, God still loves you, not only because He made you, but also because He has bought your salvation through the death of His Son. Even when the winds of money, pleasure, or ambition carry you far away from God, He never once quits hoping, longing, or working for your return.

Epilogue

During the 1970s when the Viet Nam controversy was at its zenith and the question of amnesty for draft-dodgers was ripping the country apart, a Boston radio talk-show host interviewed comedian Jerry Clower. After some light conversation, the host suddenly announced to the audience, "When we come back from this break, Jerry will tell us what he thinks of amnesty." Ninety seconds later, Jerry was forced to respond.

"Now, let's see," Jerry drawled. "Are we talking about your boy or my boy? If it's your boy, let's leave him in that foreign country where he ran. But if it's my boy, I'd just as soon he come home."[1]

As I pen the final words of this book, I'm sitting in a hotel room in Jerusalem, reflecting upon one of the most meaningful days of my life. Most Christians who travel to Israel will say that the highlight of their trip is the visit to Gethsemene or Golgotha or the empty tomb. But for me, the journey to the courtyard of Caiaphas was the most significant, perhaps because I've dwelled on this book for so long. You might remember that it was in that courtyard that Peter denied the Lord not just once or twice but three different times. Standing in that hillside courtyard and considering Peter's dramatic failure, I couldn't help but remember my own years of disobedience that kept me in the far country for so long. How could Christ ever forgive Peter? How could He ever forgive me?

How grateful I am that not too far from that hillside courtyard stands another hill where Peter's failure, my failure, and yours were forever erased. If the cross of Jesus Christ means anything it is this: No matter how far you've run, no matter how great the distance between you and God, you have a forgiving Father who stands with hands outstretched saying, "Come home."

Study Guide

Here's a study guide to help you and/or your group not only review the material in each chapter but also apply God's truth to your life. Read a chapter, then work through the corresponding set of questions, taking the time necessary for honestly answering each question. Some of the questions are extremely personal; you may choose not to share your responses with others.

CHAPTER 1: A FAMILIAR STORY

1. Which of the descriptions at the beginning of the chapter most applies to you?

2. Do you identify more with Tom or Debbie? Why?

3. In one sentence, explain how "the hunger of the wilderness" described by A. W. Tozer applies to our spiritual lives.

4. Do you agree with the author that the prodigal son story applies primarily to Christians? Why or why not?

5. Near the end of the chapter is a list of ways *Coming Home* can help you reclaim your spiritual vitality. Of the items on this list, which one interests you the most? Why?

6. Complete the following sentence: "I wish my relationship with God were more…"

7. Read Luke 15:11–31 in a different translation than the one you usually use. Give a one-sentence description of each of the major characters.

The younger son:

The older son:

The father:

8. Complete the following thought: "I hope this book will help me..."

CHAPTER 2: PRONE TO WANDER

1. Explain the contradiction of a Christian desiring to "leave the God I love."

2. What advantage did the first-century disciples enjoy over believers today? What, if any, advantages do we enjoy over those first-century believers?

3. Summarize the two truths found in Ephesians 6:23. Which one of those truths most impacts you? Why?

4. What life-areas would your mate or best friend identify as your most vulnerable points for Satan's attacks?

5. What three basic desires does Satan use to lure a believer from God? Which one is the greatest source of temptation for you? Why?

6. What are the practical benefits of understanding the reality of our sin nature?

7. Imagine that you are Satan. In a few sentences, describe the personalized scheme or strategy you'd develop for your own destruction. For example, complete the following sentence "The way I would destroy (insert your name) would be by…"

CHAPTER 3: MONEY MANIA

1. What makes money such an attractive idol?

2. Which of the four qualities of money most appeals to you? Why?

3. What does it mean to worship money? In what specific way did the rich fool worship money? Have you ever been tempted to worship money in that way? If so, when?

4. Do you agree or disagree that the idea of retirement as we know it today is both unbiblical and harmful? Why?

5. Briefly describe someone you know (without using his or her name) who illustrates how money can lead a person into "foolish and harmful desires."

6. What problems do you believe money could solve in your life? What challenges do you face that no amount of money could solve?

7. Many of our attitudes toward money are instilled at childhood. What misconceptions about money did you learn from your parents? What positive truths about money did they teach you?

8. On a scale from 1 to 10 (1 being lowest and 10 being highest), how vulnerable are you to Satan using money to lure you away from God? Why?

CHAPTER 4: MONEY SENSE

1. The author writes, "The track record for people using wealth without worshiping it isn't great." Do you know a wealthy person who has success-fully resisted the temptation to worship money? If so, describe some practical ways this person has kept him- or herself from becoming consumed by money.

2. Are you a spender or a saver? What about your mate? What are the advantages and disadvantages of each tendency?

3. The author differentiates between saving money and hoarding money. What's a reasonable savings goal for your family? After you reach that amount, what steps can you take to protect yourself from becoming a hoarder?

4. Identify some special ministry needs to which you might want to contribute in the next twelve months.

5. List some practical ways you can teach your children to have a healthy and biblical attitude toward money.

6. To help you maintain a biblical attitude toward money, memorize 1 Timothy 6:6–10.

CHAPTER 5: ADDICTED TO PLEASURE

1. According to the author, what are the two main reasons Christians become victims of Satan's attacks?

2. This chapter reminds us that Satan enters our lives subtly, not blatantly. Describe an experience in your life that illustrates this truth.

3. Summarize the biblical view of pleasure. Under what circumstances is pleasure wrong?

4. Which of the above dangers of pleasure presents you with the greatest struggle? Why?

5. Review your answers to the questions under the "It becomes our life-focus" heading. According to your responses, have you allowed pleasure to become your life-focus?

6. Describe the relationship between addiction to pleasure and immorality.

CHAPTER 6: LESSONS FROM THE PENTATHLON

1. What does it mean to "remove any excess weight"? Do you have relationships, habits, or attitudes that you need to remove? Explain.

2. How would you respond to the person who says, "God is responsible for removing sin from my life. For me to try to deal with my sin is to 'act in the flesh'"?

3. Identify one harmless pleasure you can say no to each day for a week.

4. What areas in your life receive too much of your energy? In which areas do you expend too little effort? Identify one specific change you can make in each of those areas.

5. Formulate one specific goal for each of the seven major life-areas the author mentions. Remember, an effective goal needs to be measurable. For example, "I want to read my Bible thirty minutes a day, five days a week, beginning this Monday."

Spiritual health:

Physical health:

Vocation:

Family:

Finances:

Social life:

Personal growth:

CHAPTER 7: DECLARATIONS OF INDEPENDENCE

1. Explain how the desire for success is like the desires for money and pleasure.

2. What was wrong with Satan's "goals" as described in Isaiah 14:12–14? Where and how do you see those "goals" expressed in today's culture?

3. According to the author, when does ambition become an idol? Do you have a goal that has become an idol? Explain.

4. How would you answer a person who says, "I believe that goal setting is a humanistic exercise that fails to consider God's will"? Why would you respond that way?

5. At the end of the chapter, the author asks three questions to help you evaluate whether your ambition is out of balance. Based on your answers, do you need to make any changes to achieve a new balance in your life regarding your ambition? If so, what?

6. To help you maintain a biblical attitude toward ambition, memorize Jeremiah 45:5.

CHAPTER 8: IF IT'S GOING TO BE, IT'S UP TO...HIM

1. According to this chapter, what's a life-purpose statement? Have you developed a one-sentence life-purpose statement? If so, what is it?

2. Of the seven major life-areas mentioned in the "Maintain balance in your life" section, which ones receive too much of your attention? To which ones do you need to devote more attention? List some specific steps of action you can take to achieve balance in your life.

3. Identify the one ambition that you have most difficulty surrendering to God's sovereignty. If God said no to that ambition, what need in your life are you afraid would go unfulfilled?

4. According to the author, what basic misunderstanding about the father caused the younger son to leave home? Have you ever had the same misunderstanding about God's plan for your life? Explain.

5. Psalm 37:4–5 says, "Delight yourself in the LORD; and He will give you the desires of your heart. Commit your way to the LORD, trust also in Him, and He will do it." Paraphrase these verses in your own words. Now commit these verses to memory.

CHAPTER 9: THE TRUTH ABOUT SIN

1. Refer to the self-discovery questions near the beginning of the chapter. Based on your answers to those questions, how would you summarize the condition of your spiritual life at this time?

2. How do you feel about the condition of your spiritual life? Why?

3. Do you agree or disagree with the statement that life in the far country is not all pain? Why or why not?

4. Reread Psalm 32:3–4. Have you ever felt the same sensations? If so, when?

5. Do you believe that a Christian should ever fear God? Why or why not?

6. Can you recall a period in your life when you saw God's patience demonstrated? If so, when?

7. What important lessons have you learned about God while living in the far country?

8. Imagine sitting down for a cup of coffee with a friend or family member who is living in the far country. What would you say to that person if he or she was happy with life and saw no need to change?

CHAPTER 10: INTERVENTION

1. How is God different from the father in the prodigal son story? How does this difference make you feel about God?

2. According to the Bible, what are some of the reasons that people experience suffering? Can we always identify the cause of suffering? Why or why not?

3. Why is financial hardship such an effective reproof? Have you ever experienced this kind of reproof? If so, what specific lessons did you learn from it?

4. Of the three different reproofs the author mentions, which kind would most likely get your attention? Why?

5. The author states sometimes God uses cancer, heart disease, and AIDS as a form of discipline in a Christian's life. Do you agree or disagree? Use Scripture to support your answer.

6. Have you ever been tempted to think that you are exempt from God's correction? If so, why?

7. Identify a Christian you know who has experienced God's discipline. What lessons can you learn from this person's experience.

8. Carefully examine your own life for a moment. Could you label as reproofs any difficulties you're experiencing? Do you have any areas of your life that you know displease God? What specific steps of action can you take to change?

CHAPTER 11: THE JOURNEY HOME

1. What are some of the barriers that might have kept the prodigal son from returning home to his father? As you think about your life and your relationship with God, what issues might prevent your return?

2. Describe a crisis that you can now reflect upon with "particular satisfaction." Why can you do so?

3. Describe a current problem in your life that you can't understand. Do you think God is disciplining you? Why or why not?

4. Contrast the popular understanding of repentance with the biblical definition.

5. As you look back over your life, what experiences do you most regret? Why?

6. Has this chapter taught you anything about repentance that could have erased those regrets? If so, what?

7. The author says that "true repentance always results in definitive action." List one positive change you could make in each of the following life-areas.

Marriage:

Parenting:

Friendships:

Time management:

Moral purity:

Relationship with God:

CHAPTER 12: THE WAITING FATHER

1. What words or images immediately come to mind whenever you think of God?

2. Why do you think so many people find it difficult to picture God as a forgiving Father?

3. Can you recall an incident in which you experienced the undeserved forgiveness of a parent? If so, describe that experience.

4. How well are you modeling God's forgiveness to your children? How can a parent balance discipline with grace?

5. What truths about God did the Pharisees understand correctly? What did they misunderstand about Him? Given Jesus' response to the Pharisees, how should we react to "Pharisees" we encounter today?

6. Does God overlook our sin? Why or why not?

7. Which sins do you have the most difficulty believing God could forgive either in yourself or in others? What has this chapter taught you about God's forgiveness?

8. "Christians don't need to confess their sins since they have already been forgiven." Do you agree or disagree with this statement? Why?

9. Do you have failures in your life that you need to acknowledge to God? Why not take a moment right now to identify and confess those shortcomings, knowing that you have a forgiving Father who is ready to listen?

Chapter 13: The Morning After

1. In one sentence, summarize the theme of this chapter.

2. Have you ever recommitted your life to God but found yourself unable to maintain that new commitment? If so, what factors kept you from fulfilling your recommitment?

3. Why doesn't God erase all the consequences of our sin when we ask for His forgiveness? Relate your answer to a consequence of sin you may be experiencing now.

4. Suppose someone comes to you for counsel. A mate or parent has deeply hurt this person. He or she says, "I will forgive this person only if he (or she) asks for my forgiveness and starts treating me differently." How would you respond? Does the Bible teach conditional or unconditional forgiveness? Explain.

5. Are you living in the "far country" now? If not, have you ever been there? In a paragraph, summarize how it feels to live apart from God.

6. List three specific steps of action you will take to make your devotional time more consistent and productive.

7. Reflect on each of the three major sections in this book, and list one truth from each section that deeply impressed you.

The Departure (chapters 1–8):

Life in the Far Country (chapters 9–10):

The Return (chapters 11–Epilogue):

8. Complete this sentence: "As a result of this study, I am going to…"

Notes

CHAPTER 1: A FAMILIAR STORY

1. A. W. Tozer, *The Root of the Righteous* (Harrisburg, Pa.: Christian Publications, Inc., 1955), 100.

2. Ron Mehl, *Meeting God at a Dead End* (Sisters, Ore.: Questar Publishers, Inc., 1996), 210–5.

CHAPTER 2: PRONE TO WANDER

1. Charles R. Swindoll, *Simple Faith* (Dallas: Word Publishing, 1991), 166–7.

2. Howard G. Hendricks, *Taking a Stand* (Portland, Ore.: Multnomah Press, 1972), 59.

3. Charles C. Ryrie, ed., *The Ryrie Study Bible,* New American Standard translation (Chicago: Moody Press, 1976), 1862.

4. Charles Colson, *Loving God* (Grand Rapids, Mich.: Zondervan Publishing, 1983), 103.

5. Robert Jeffress, *Heaven Can't Wait* (Nashville: Broadman and Holman Publishers, 1995), 34.

CHAPTER 3: MONEY MANIA

1. Howard L. Dayton Jr., *Your Money: Frustration or Freedom* (Wheaton, Ill.: Tyndale House Publishers, Inc., 1971), 99.

2. Tom Maurstad, *Dallas Morning News,* 8 June 1996, C1.

CHAPTER 4: MONEY SENSE

1. Mark Galli, "Saint Nasty," *Christianity Today,* 17 June 1996, 25–6.

2. Dallas Willard, *The Spirit of the Disciplines* (San Francisco: Harper and Row Publishers, 1988), 197.

3. Ibid.

4. Robert Jeffress, *Guilt-Free Living* (Wheaton, Ill.: Tyndale House Publishers, Inc., 1995), 64.

CHAPTER 5: ADDICTED TO PLEASURE

1. Haddon W. Robinson, ed., *Biblical Sermons* (Grand Rapids, Mich.: Baker Book House Company, 1989), 17.

2. Willard, *The Spirit of the Disciplines,* 79.

3. Peter H. Brown, *Marilyn: The Last Take* (New York: Nal Dutton, 1992), 50–51.

4. Quoted in Steve Farrar, *Finishing Strong* (Sisters, Ore.: Questar Publishers, 1995), 82.

5. Ibid.

CHAPTER 6: LESSONS FROM THE PENTATHLON

1. John MacArthur Jr., *The MacArthur New Testament Commentary: 1 Corinthians* (Chicago: Moody Press, 1984), 215.

2. Joe L. Wall, *Going for the Gold* (Chicago: Moody Press, 1991), 74–5.

CHAPTER 7: DECLARATIONS OF INDEPENDENCE

1. Napoleon Hill, *Think and Grow Rich* (New York: A Fawcett Crest Book published by Ballantine Books, 1960), 35.

2. Tim Hansel, *Holy Sweat* (Waco, Tex.: Word Books, 1987), 129–30.

3. Charles R. Swindoll, *Hand Me Another Brick* (Nashville: Thomas Nelson Publishers, 1978), 190–1.

4. Erwin W. Lutzer, *The Serpent of Paradise* (Chicago: Moody Press, 1996), 31.

5. Adapted from Donald T. Philipps, *Lincoln on Leadership* (New York: Warner Books, 1992), 32.

CHAPTER 8: IF IT'S GOING TO BE, IT'S UP TO…HIM

1. Quoted in Stephen R. Covey, A. Roger Merrill, and Rebecca R. Merrill, *First Things First* (New York: Simon and Schuster, 1994), 49.

CHAPTER 9: THE TRUTH ABOUT SIN

1. A. W. Tozer, *The Pursuit of God* (Camp Hill, Pa.: Christian Publications, Inc., 1982), 37.

CHAPTER 10: INTERVENTION

1. Bill Hybels, *Descending into Greatness* (Grand Rapids, Mich.: Zondervan Publishing, 1993), 48.

CHAPTER 12: THE WAITING FATHER

1. Philip Yancey, *Finding God in Unexpected Places* (Nashville: Moorings, a division of the Ballantine Publishing Group, Random House, Inc., 1995), 180.

2. Quoted in John MacArthur Jr., *The Love of God* (Dallas: Word Publishing, 1996), 41.

CHAPTER 13: THE MORNING AFTER

1. Quoted in Charles R. Swindoll, *Hope Again* (Dallas: Word Publishing, 1996), 199.

2. Michael P. Green, *Illustrations for Biblical Preaching* (Grand Rapids, Mich.: Baker Book House, 1982), 153.

3. Swindoll, *Hope Again,* 38–9.

4. Donald K. Campbell, *Daniel: Decoder of Dreams* (Wheaton, Ill.: Victor Books, 1977), 49.

5. Some of these ideas were adapted from *Guilt-Free Living* by Robert Jeffress (Wheaton, Ill.: Tyndale House Publishers, 1995), 193–204.

EPILOGUE

1. Jimmy Allen, *Burden of a Secret* (Nashville: Moorings, a division of the Ballantine Publishing Group, Random House, Inc., 1995), 111.

Also available
from **Robert Jeffress**

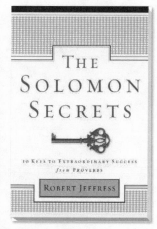

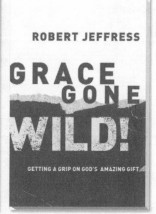

🦌 WATERBROOK PRESS
www.waterbrookpress.com